Contemporary IT Service Delivery in Enterprise

Handbook for Service Delivery Managers

Jagadeshwar Gattu
Prafull Verma
Kalyan Kumar

Copyright © 2018
Jagadeshwar Gattu, Prafull Verma, and Kalyan Kumar
All rights reserved.

June 2019

ISBN-13: 978-0578466187

All trademarks, brand names and product names and titles referenced in this book are trade and brand names, trademarks, product names, copy-rights or other intellectual property rights of their respective holders.

In addition to the registered trademarks, many of the designations are used by product vendors and other organizations to distinguish their product and services and may be claimed as the trademark or service marks. Authors acknowledge such designations and used those designations including trademarks, in initial caps or all caps.

ACKNOWLEDGMENTS

Ever since I have been into infrastructure service delivery management, and from the moment I assumed the role of a service delivery manager, I realized that it is an art and science of dealing with people and technology. As I grew in the organization, I wanted to share my learnings and experience. This book is my first attempt to do so.

I would like to thank all the team members who worked with me for the last 15 years and inspired me to realize the need to create a publication like this. I would also like to thank both Kalyan & Prafull for hearing this idea and coming forward to collectively complete this project.

Finally, I would also like to thank my wife Aparna & my sons Shreyash and Havish for encouraging me and giving me time and support to complete this work.

Jagadeshwar Gattu

This project was initiated by Jagadeshwar Gattu, popularly known as Jags amongst colleagues. He is always full of guidance to his large team of service delivery managers worldwide. When he told me about his idea of a handbook for service delivery managers, and invited to contribute, it sounded very appealing to me and I thankfully accepted.

In fact, Kalyan Kumar (popularly known as KK amongst colleagues) and I have had several ideas that have been published in the past and some of these have resonated to Jags in the context of service delivery management. It was therefore a good idea to come forward and contribute towards this publication, and I am thankful to Jags who made it very easy for me to contribute by precisely defining the context for my contribution and also glad that it was found useful.

Like all such projects in past, my wife Annie supported and it was a special gesture, especially as we became empty nesters this summer.

Special Thanks to Varun Vijaykumar and Ashish Joseph for reviewing this handbook and making certain updates to improve the overall quality.

Prafull Verma

This book is the culmination of several extensive debates based on real ground situations we saw in the Infrastructure Service Delivery space, both from an enterprise customer and a managed service provider's perspective. I am really looking forward to insights from the SDM community on how they will apply this into their daily routine and give us more closed loop feedback to create additional content in the future.

Like all our previous books, special mention to my better half Zulfia and my boy Azlan who gave me time, inspiration and also acted as sounding boards and helped in keeping my 'curious' side turned on.

Kalyan Kumar

FOREWORD

Service delivery management is a complex discipline that involves variety of technologies and uses technology to manage technologies.

But it is also business management because it involves cost and resource management. It is also quality management because customers demand and pay for quality. It is also people management because people are working for servicing people. It is also customer relationship management because service delivery and service consumption involve customer interactions. You can keep on expanding what it is and conclude that it is a bit if everything in a typical business but for a specific segment of IT Service.

This is probably the first book truly targeted at service delivery managers in IT Services outsourcing organization. There are abundant handbooks available in technology area, published by not only the originator of the technology product but also by the practitioners of particular technology. However, service delivery management is not just technology management, so for a service delivery manager, there is a vacuum and this book is an attempt to fill that void.

The authors of this handbook form a unique combination of experience.

Jagadeshwar runs multibillion-dollar service delivery for a large IT services Provider. Kalyan is the business technologist with deep architectural and product/offering expertise. Prafull is the service management practitioner with product development in his domain. Together, that covers the majority of aspects of managing services produced by technology.

I am not surprised to note that the book is largely based on the context of outsourcing management because of background of the organization from where the authors are coming from. Nevertheless, there is guidance beyond outsourcing, such as SIAM and service level management that is included. The authors promise that the future edition of this book will expand this role across lines of business and may be for insourced service SDM as well. There is valuable reading material for customers also!

The handbook is written with the consideration that a service delivery manager needs to understand all these aspects and be a generalist rather than a specialist. Each topic is explained with a common-sense approach and will be useful for anybody engaged in IT services. The arrangement of topics indicates the experience of the authors. For example, the chapter that discusses the hygiene of the operation laid out with 80-20 rule. These six areas address the 80 percent of the operation excellence. While teaching an SDM how to deliver good service, it also provides clues to customers on how to obtain good service. In fact, this book is a good reading for anyone who is engaged in IT service in any role.

Happy reading!!

Rhonda Vetere
Chief Information Officer
Santander Bank

TABLE OF CONTENT

1 INTRODUCTION — 01
    1.1 Evolution Of IT Landscape & It Services In Enterprises — 01
    1.2 Enterprise IT World — 03
    1.3 Modern Vs. Contemporary IT Landscape — 05
    1.4 Future Landscape & Future IT Organization — 06
        1.4.1 Blueprint for the Digital Foundation — 19
        1.4.2 Blueprint For The Digital Foundation — 21

2 OUTSOURCING OF IT SERVICES — 23
    2.1 Evolution Of Outsourcing — 23
    2.2 Business Case For Outsourcing — 24
    2.3 Customer's Faulty Perspective On Service Delivery — 26

3 THE SERVICE DELIVERY MANAGER (SDM) — 30
    3.1 Typical Day in the Life of SDM — 33
    3.2 SDM: Who are You? — 34
    3.3 SDM: Why are you in this position? — 35
    3.4 SDM: What is Expected from You? — 37
        3.4.1 General Operations — 37
        3.4.2 Embed Service Management with Technology Management — 45

    3.4.3 Team Management — 47
  3.5 Essential Soft Skills for SDM — 53
  3.6 Human Failure: Errors and Violations — 57
    3.6.1 Understanding and Avoiding Human Error — 59
    3.6.2 Understanding and Avoiding Human Violations — 61
    3.6.3 Doer & Checker Process — 63
  3.7 Contract Renewals — 63
  3.8 Role of SDM in Transition — 64
  3.9 IT Service Quality Gaps — 69
    3.9.1 Other Factors that Impact Service Quality — 78
  3.10 SLO - The Early Operations Period — 78

4 SERVICE OPERATIONS — 80
  4.1 Process — 80
    4.1.1 Process Thinking — 82
    4.1.2 Process Thinking — 84
    4.1.3 Process Maintenance — 86
    4.1.4 Why Processes Fail? — 88
    4.1.5 Generally Observed Process Deficiencies — 95
  4.2 Function — 116
    4.2.1 Service Desk: Most Visible Function — 116
    4.2.2 Other Functions Embedded in Processes — 117
  4.3 Tools — 118

5 KEY HYGIENES OF OPERATIONAL HEALTH — 119
  5.1 Event Monitoring and Control — 119
  5.2 Patch Management — 122
  5.3 Batch Management — 125
  5.4 Incident Management & Critical Incident Management — 127
  5.5 Backup and Restore — 131
  5.6 DR Management — 132

6 SERVICE DELIVERY IN MULTISOURCE ENVIRONMENT 134
    6.1.1 Need for Service Integration & Management (SIAM) 136
    6.1.2 SIAM Vs CFS 143

7 SERVICE LEVEL MANAGEMENT 150
    7.1 Developing and Managing SLA 152
        7.1.1 SLA Architecture for SLA Gap Analysis 153
    7.2 Customer Relationship Management 155

8 APPENDIX 160
    8.1 Technical Analyst Role In Service Management Processes 160

1 INTRODUCTION

1.1 Evolution of IT Landscape & IT Services in Enterprises

Computers in business started with mainframe when computers were deemed as 'business machines' not as technological equipment. The name of the company that produced computers made it clear that even though it was a technical equipment, it ultimately was a business machine. Mainframes were considered a state-of-the-art 'technology' in this era.

The prominent programming language was COBOL (Common Business-Oriented Language), again the word 'business' in COBOL was an integral part and served a purpose. Mainframes and later superminis with terminals (now referred to as 'dumb terminals') were forming the IT landscape.

The word IT was non-existent, and it was referred to as MIS (Management Information System). Line printers, reel-to-reel magnetic tape drives and large Winchester hard drives were attached to mainframe or superminis. During this time, it was always the batch processing and the maintenance was dominated by hardware maintenance. Only large organizations could afford computer systems then. A prominent trend during this time was to choose a vendor – IBM, DEC and HP among others who dominated the era. Enterprise success was completely dependent on the worthiness of the chosen vendor.

Things however changed with time. The emergence of 'Information

Technology' formed the modern world of enterprise IT – it started with desktop, client server, and distributed computing. However, this is also when IT troubles started as IT people started focusing on technology elements as opposed to business services.

This was the late 80s when personal computers proliferated into smaller organizations and departments of large organizations. This was the era of PC LANs and PC networking.

The modern world of IT took an interesting turn with the proliferation of the Internet. It was a business compulsion for enterprises to move towards an e-commerce strategy, leading to the integration of existing Enterprise Information Systems (EIS) with new web-based applications.

Enterprises were forced to extend the reach of their EIS systems to support Business-to-Business (B2B) transactions. J2EE became the dominant architecture in the early 2000s. Before the J2EE Connector architecture was defined, no specification for the Java platform addressed the problem of providing a standard architecture for integrating heterogeneous EIS systems. Examples of EIS systems include ERP, mainframe transaction processing, database systems and legacy applications not written in the Java programming language.

Most EIS vendors and application server vendors used non-standard, vendor-specific architecture, to provide connectivity between application servers and EIS. By defining a set of scalable, secure, and transactional mechanisms, the J2EE connector architecture enabled the integration of EISs with application servers and enterprise applications. Along with J2EE, Microsoft .Net framework also started to make its presence in the enterprises and became a strong competing alternative. Although legacy systems today, both of these form a major part of the legacy enterprise application landscape.

The contemporary enterprise IT world is focused on Cloud Computing and cloud native services. All new applications are getting built and deployed using the cloud native model. Traditional datacenters are moving towards retirement and SDDC model in the form of private cloud is picking up as a viable alternative to run on premise applications. However, these applications are also getting re-architected using cloud native architecture.

1.2 Enterprise IT World

Traditionally, enterprise IT world was established around the datacenters as a 'service-producing factory'. The size of this factory was dependent on the size and the industry of the enterprise. Enterprises had multiple service-producing factories that delivered those services through the network connections to the end points.

Today, these service-producing factories are scaling down and moving to cloud. In-house factories are also getting modernized using software defined data center technology. Servers (and associated software) in datacenter are service-producing CIs and all user devices are service consumption end points. This brings in an important concept of service delivery and service support.

Service Delivery vs. Service Support

IT service delivery refers to the kind of service where there is no direct interaction between the service producer and service receiver. Services are produced by machines and delivered to receivers via network channels on the receiver's devices.

Of course, there are people at both ends. At the service-production end, people operate the machines that produce the service. At the receiver's end, a person interacts with their device to use the service. Thus, IT service delivery is essentially machine-to-machine interaction, with a person behind the machine at each end.

1 INTRODUCTION

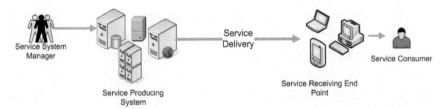

Figure 1: Service Delivery—Machine-to-Machine Relationship with People Behind Machine

In ITIL V2, availability management, capacity management, and service-level management processes are the key service-delivery processes. As we can see in Figure 1, machines perform the prime activity of service delivery while people (service providers) manage those machines.

This situation gives relatively clear definitions of standards and targets. Processes of production can be effective and leave little scope of deviation from written specifications. Quality is relatively easy to define and achieve. The quality of this aspect of service is 'technical quality': for example, measuring what the customer received when the service was delivered.

The complexity is related to the technology and hard skills that are required for quality delivery. The quality dimensions are reliability, efficiency, performance, completeness, integrity, fault tolerance and tangibility.

A major part of Service-level Agreements (SLAs) is devoted to defining these aspects of services because these are definable. Also, most of service-level management activities are focused on this aspect because they are do-able.

On the other hand, 'service support' refers to the kind of service where there is a direct interaction between the service provider and the service receiver. This need usually arises when the service receiver is not able to use the service.

Inability to use does not necessarily mean the service is interrupted, and service support acts as a catalyst to restore the service delivery.

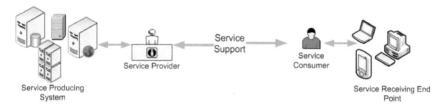

Figure 2: Service Support—People-to-People Relationship with Machine Behind

In ITIL V2, incident management, problem management, and change management are the key service-support processes. People perform the prime activity of service support, and the customer directly receives the benefit. Here people are dealing with people while machines are in the background. Even though it is ITIL V3 now, the fundamental processes which can be implemented remain the same.

1.3 Modern vs. Contemporary IT Landscape

The modern IT era is all about client server and internet. Unlike modern design, which represents a time period, contemporary design is dynamic and constantly changing.

By definition 'contemporary' means 'belonging to or occurring in the present'. Contemporary technology reflects what is new or popular at the time. This is the cloud native world.

Today, the enterprise landscape is primarily based on monolithic client-server architecture of applications with additional Web enablement layer added after the proliferation of Internet. The shift in emphasis when it comes to IT architecture is reflected below:

- Natively designed cloud applications running in cloud (increasing in landscape).
- Cloud-enabled applications running on managed IaaS Cloud (big momentum)
- Legacy applications running in unmanaged IaaS cloud (increasing).
- Legacy application in legacy infrastructure (decreasing).

1 INTRODUCTION

1.4 Future Landscape & Future IT Organization

In the 21st century, IT is embedded everywhere. It would be appropriate to use the term Service Management (SM) rather than IT Service Management

Interestingly, the industry that claims to adopt and follow advanced trends in technology turns a blind eye in the area of SM and continues to practice decades old legacy systems. Besides, the way enterprises approach service management is perfectly suited for a world that does not exist.

In this new world, XaaS is the new delivery model, and the industry warrants new approaches to service management. XaaS is a collective term that is said to stand for a number of things, including 'X as a service,' where X can stand for everything (and anything).

This is a rapidly expanding model that grew from a utility-based service model and is applied to IT, and now non-IT services as well. XaaS is the essence of cloud computing, and the most common examples of XaaS are Software as a Service (SaaS), Infrastructure as a Service (IaaS) and Platform as a Service (PaaS).

Old World	XaaS world
Monolithic application infrastructure	Cloud infrastructure
Service is produced by CIs	Service is composed by *microservices*
Technology management mindset with focus on system architecture and system Integration	Outcome management mindset with focus on service architecture and service Integration

Old World	XaaS world
CMDB is the center of ITSM world around which everything revolves	Service Catalog is the center of service-management world around which everything Revolves
Service provider with technology based internal groups and external supplier	Service-based organization with service supply chain with new roles (e.g. creator, operator, provider, broker, integrator, etc.) OLA and UC concept are not applicable
SLA dictated by customer.	SLA dictated by service provider.

Table 1: Difference between Old World and XaaS World

Technology Spending Rising Yet, CIO Budget Shrinking

About 15 years ago approximately 80% of enterprise technology spending was under the control of CIO and web enablement was at its peak.

CIOs could not handle the business demand because of two reasons. Firstly, their focus was on technology management, and they were slipping on business alignment.

Secondly, business demand was overwhelmingly high to handle. In fact, IT outsourcing for infrastructure got momentum during this era. As a result, business looked at alternate supply. Shadow IT started growing, and so did the ASPs of the world.

This trend continued and ASPs advanced to the next level of being SaaS providers. Business is directly sourcing IT in the form of SaaS and pointed solutions, bypassing the CIO and creating their own shadow IT with third parties. Therefore, the CIO's share of enterprise technology spending is now less than 20%.

If the CIOs do not radically change their strategy, they will continue to lose their empire bit by bit. Besides, they are facing the pressure of deliberate cost reductions. Businesses, on the other hand, are paying premium to external providers for agility and business-aligned services that are largely cloud-based.

The Relevance of ITIL

ITIL V2 and Windows XP were released in 2001. While Windows XP is out of support and a dead product now, ITIL is still being used across enterprises. The approach to deliver and manage services has not been able to keep pace with dynamic technological developments.

Let's have a look at other disruptions. Where was VMware in 2001? What about cloud? There was no virtualization or cloud then, the enterprise IT infrastructure was monolithic, based on client server architecture. ITIL was primarily designed for an environment that was largely static.

One may argue that ITIL V3 was released in 2008, but the truth is that the historical ITIL V2 practices of incident management, change management, and CMDB among others that form the major practice area in the ITIL implementation still remain the same.

Today's enterprise IT environment is highly virtualized and also moving to cloud. Therefore, the traditional ITIL practices do not hold relevance. For example, enterprises dynamically move the machine from one host to another using vMotion and also scale up or down node in a cluster using auto-scale feature of vRealize, and the need for an RFC is totally eliminated.

They also do not need several controls prescribed in ITIL for software license compliance because they are consuming SaaS and not buying the license. In other words, the relevance of ITIL is diminishing as rapidly as the monolithic IT infrastructure is shrinking.

However, enterprises are still obsessed with ITIL. In a typical ITIL theme, service providers are internal support groups and external service providers. In the XaaS world, this is replaced by service supply chain with new roles such as service creator, service operator, service provider, and service broker and service integrator.

Also, ITIL was designed with the functional structure of tower-based organization that are serving to business customers. Today in the DevOps world, development, operation, and business work as one team. In all, ITIL needs radical transformation to meet the requirements of todays' enterprises.

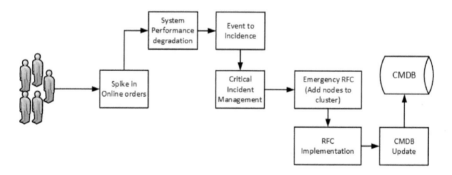

Figure 3: Old school of ITIL

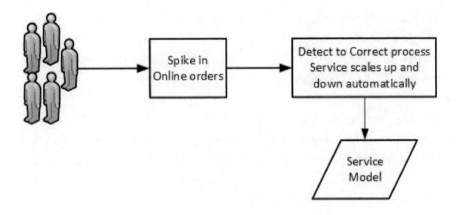

Figure 4: New School of Cloud

The Generation of Born Digital

Traditional customers are being replaced by a new generation of millennials referred to as 'born digital' users. A large number of users in the enterprise are 'digital settlers'- people who may not be born with today's technologies, yet adopted it very well.

This has resulted in a dramatic change in the profile of service consumers with born digital users and digital settlers forming the majority. Digital immigrants who are baffled with today's technology and continue to use old way of working are now the minority.

Therefore, the question is, who your real customers are and where you should focus.

Moreover, the responsibility of building and rolling out services is often left to the digital immigrants in the organization who see things from their point of view rather than the point of view of the new generation. We need to understand that today users consume service on demand, anytime, from anywhere and any device; they demand for a true self service experience.

User Support Is Out & Service Support Is In

Service support for the subscribed service and not for 'me as a person' is the key perspective as well as the expectations of the new-generation service consumer.

There is a big difference between user support and service support. In service support mode, the support boundary has a specific warranty and utility. In the user support mode, there is no boundary and support can span across multiple services. For example, if you have an issue with the Internet service, then you call your Internet service provider. Similarly, if there is an issue with your laptop, then you call your equipment seller or you fix it yourself.

However, the modern world service is designed for self-service, not human-assisted service. Relying on the user support with helpdesk for user experience is not viable.

Take the example of enterprise e-mail service versus Google Gmail service. Typically, an enterprise will produce e-mail service using a cluster of MS exchange servers and AD servers. Of late, it has moved into the cloud with Office 365, but the helpdesk support for e-mail is still required. Typically, an enterprise of 50,000 users will have four to five persons on service desk to support e-mail, attachment, and One-Drive-related issues.

On the other hand, Gmail (and Google drive) that has a user base of 1.5 billion, anytime service, anywhere on any device without any restrictions operates without any service desk whatsoever, and the user experience is still far superior. This is possible because Google has built the service for user experience by design, not by relying on assisted support.

Service Catalog Becomes the Core of Service Management

In the ITIL world, CMDB was the center of the ITSM universe around which everything revolved. The theme was that the service is produced by a configuration item (application CI, server CI, and database CI to name a few). Since the CIs were related to one another, we needed the CMDB to understand and manage the service.

In the modern world, a service is essential in a XaaS model and is composed of micro services, and each micro service is independent.

ITIL promoted the idea of CMDB in the year 2002 and as we mentioned in the first section, it has become outdated now. In the era of XaaS, a service is composed by micro services and each micro service is independent.

Service catalog brings in standardization and quality. If a service is published in the catalog, it is available according to the specifications published. Besides, personalization is allowed as much as the service provider allows. So, customization is out and personalization is in.

CMDB is therefore deep down in the value chain, while the service catalog has moved to the top of the value chain.

Crowdsourcing is the Key

The ubiquity of networked people inside and outside enterprises has changed the collaboration and communication radically. The 'mobile population' is debating, discussing, and collaborating all the time through multiple channels within and outside the enterprise.

One very good illustration will be the use of crowdsourcing for knowledge management. Enterprises are spending a lot of money on building knowledge bases for IT support. A typical knowledge-management system includes processes to source, verify, authorize and publish knowledge and this is carried out by designated roles such as knowledge contributor, SME, technical writer and knowledge manager.

However, users often bypass the enterprise knowledge base and 'Google' the problem, looking for solutions on the Internet. Google returns multiple options and solutions, and the user fixes the problem by trial and error. In this scenario, crowd is the knowledge provider and crowd is the knowledge consumer. There is no guarantee that the knowledge record, which one has access to will work, but still it works better.

Enterprises will continue to build and maintain the enterprise-specific knowledge, but they also need to invest but they should also leverage the crowdsourcing model.

Software-Defined Everything

A composable infrastructure framework allows physical compute, storage, and network fabric resources as services. In a composable infrastructure, resources are logically pooled so that administrators are not required to physically configure hardware to support a specific software application. Instead, the software developer defines the application's requirements for physical infrastructure using policies and service profiles and then the software uses API calls to create the infrastructure it needs to run on bare metal, as a virtual machine or as a container.

Composable infrastructure enables an enterprise to use its own physical infrastructure in a more cost-effective manner by reducing waste and the amount of time it takes to deploy a new application.

Several vendors are promoting the concept as a way to provision workloads just as quickly and efficiently as public cloud service providers can, while still maintaining control over the infrastructure that supports mission-critical applications in a private cloud setting. The concept of pooling physical infrastructure resources and building infrastructure logically is supported by the growing popularity of Software-Defined

Networking (SDN), object storage, converged infrastructure and DevOps.

Although there are no agreed-upon standards for deploying a composable infrastructure, different vendors and proponents are describing composable infrastructure by different names – including programmable infrastructure, intelligent infrastructure, Software-defined Infrastructure (SDI), Infrastructure as Code (IaC), decoupled infrastructure and hardware disaggregation.

Legacy to Cloud Native

The CIOs' cloud strategy is mostly bottom up, starting from Infrastructure as a service (IaaS). This movement is primarily driven by the need to avoid buying new hardware or investing more on the existing hardware. Even infrastructure movement to cloud may not have the true price advantage, but it is considered to convert CAPEX to OPEX. In reality, business needs to take a top-down approach while transitioning to cloud – primarily from the SaaS side.

It is a matter of mindset. Technology-centric thinking versus business or function-centric thinking. When people are asked about 'What comes to their mind when they hear Amazon?' Most IT professionals answer that Amazon is the number one cloud provider, referring to AWS cloud. On the contrary, non-IT people talk about Amazon's retail business and even the acquisition of Whole Foods. Interesting, isn't it!

The Levels of Cloud Nativity & Migration

While IaaS cloud is commodity and not a big deal, a true cloud native business application is a big deal.

Figure 5 provides an overview of the different levels of cloud maturity. Today most organizations start at level 2 and some of them refactor applications to level 3. A few of them work on a small portion of the application portfolio up to level 4. Most of the SaaS providers are here. Level 5 is only really achieved by enterprises of the 21st century and born digital enterprises—the likes of Uber, Netflix, and Google, to name a few.

While CIOs roadmap of migration of existing application is based on the bottom-up approach, businesses are starting from the top.

1 INTRODUCTION

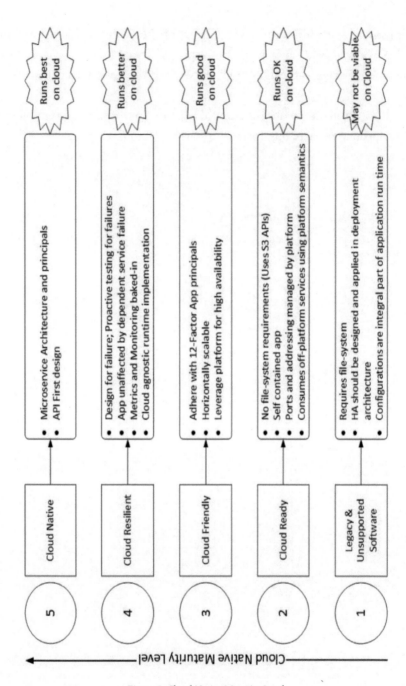

Figure 5: Cloud Native Maturity Level

Regardless of the migration approach being undertaken, there is always an element of implied service management migration that should never be ignored and should be embedded as an integral part of cloud migration. Service management migration would focus on re-engineering of service management process, tool, and function that would deal with the migrated state of the technology.

Analytics and AI-driven Automation

An interesting question to ask is 'How do Googles and Amazons of the world run their massive infrastructure? See Figure 6 to understand where error detection to error correction is completely automated, backed by the knowledge derived from the machine learning, analytics, and AI. It is not just the matter of detection and correction; these massive infrastructures also keep on updating the service very frequently. Continuous integration and deployment are also completely automated.

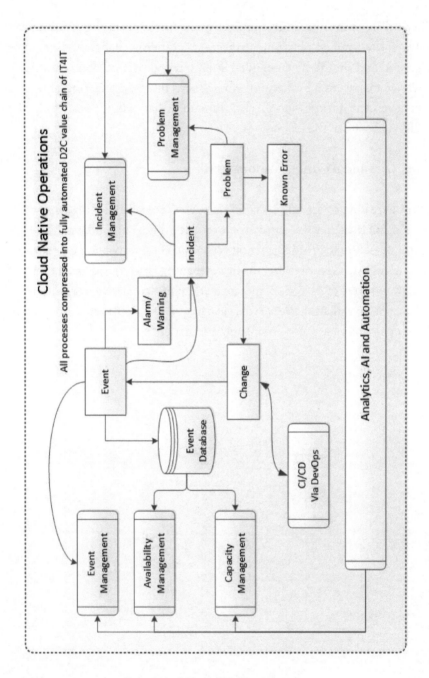

Figure 6: Analytics and AI-driven Operation

The entire service-lifecycle management in this area is being fundamentally transformed with the help of Machine Data-driven Operations.

The amount of data collected via instrumentation in IT operations is really not adding any value in terms of driving proactivity. This is due to the implementation of old rules-based management systems which need to be programmed. With complex software-defined overlays in hybrid infrastructure and cloud, container platforms and continuous delivery of applications, the old ways of human-centric operations have to give way to Machine-centric Operations, leveraging the advancement in the field of AI.

The approach towards AIOPS to be able to have a platform, which can drive the entire 'Detect to Correct' lifecycle using advances in Data Science and using advanced Machine Learning (supervised and unsupervised) applied to streams of metrics data, Neural Networks (Reinforcement Learning) for understanding patterns, graph-based nodal relationships between different entities in the digital technology landscape and Natural Language Processing (NLP) to parse logs/events and leverage cognitive conversational capability for user/service support interactions, is the vision on which AIOPS will thrive upon.

This would also lead to an adoption of 'Site/Platform Reliability Engineering' based operations rather than the old pyramid-based operations.

1.4.1 Blueprint for the Digital Foundation

Digital economy is driving the need for digital infrastructure. Next-generation IT Infrastructure would be nothing but the digital foundation of enterprise business as depicted in Figure 7.

1 INTRODUCTION

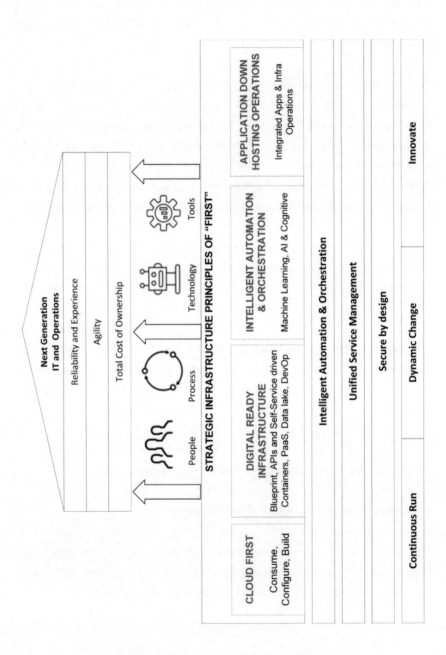

Figure 7: Next-generation Digital Foundation

What is changing in Next-Gen Infrastructure?

- Customer spend is shifting towards building the foundational capability for their Digital Enterprise and modernization of the Infrastructure
- Cloud is a means to innovate; it is not a cost saving mechanism.
- Software-defined is the new normal across datacenters, workplace, and networks.
- Platform definitions shifting to application and data infrastructure and Hybrid Cloud is the new normal.
- Employee experience and engagement using AI/Cognitive/Cloud.
- Cloud Native and SaaS based applications are driving the Digital Workplace.

What is Required by Enterprise IT to Capture This Shift:

- Build next-generation IT Blueprint for digital transformation led offerings and solutions.
- New partnerships and ecosystems.
- Alternate commercial and consumption models.
- Modernization of people skills and culture (such as Site Reliability Engineering, Infrastructure as a Code, and DevOps).
- Operations Model using AIOPS and Autonomics at the core.

1.4.2 Changes in Delivery and Support Model

Reorganizing from Tower-based Organization to Service Supply Chain-based Organization is imperative.

Develop the mindset of a service supply chain. Think what service is produced for whom. The customer could be an entity in the service supply chain. For example, "I am a server admin" is a traditional thinking whereas "I am providing reliable compute service to application builder who is also part of service supply chain to end customer" reflects the correct mindset. The service supply chain includes multiple roles in the chain – starting from service creator and ending with service consumers.

The middle of the chain will include service operator, service supporter, service provider, service integrator and service broker among others. An entity in the supply chain can assume more than one role and depending on the service, some of the roles may not be required – for example, the service integrator role is required only when the end service needs integration with another service.

The future of service delivery will focus on providing an Agile Platform, which is business driven and can adjust to the changing dynamics of digital business.

Adapting Next-Generation Service-Management Approach

The new model that revolves around the service catalog and service-management approach is also set to change. Traditional ITIL-based service-management system will gradually become obsolete as the world moves to the Cloud Native maturity model level 5 and the newer XaaS service-management systems emerge.

The shift will be towards service-oriented, dynamic, catalog-driven fulfillment of technology and business services, and service will be operated using 'reliability engineering' methods at their core.

2 Outsourcing of IT Services

2.1 Evolution of Outsourcing

The evolution of the IT outsourcing business started from the mainframe era where data processing was centralized using massive mainframe systems and associated programmers/operators who delivered the processing service.

This evolved into the distributed computing era, where datacenters were first built in-house and then got migrated to shared datacenter facilities on the outsourcers' premises and then to the shared datacenter locations owned by specialized datacenter hosting service providers.

The same happened in the desktop computing space which evolved from facilities management on premise to holistic end-user computing services and remote managed desktop and client devices.

Similarly, on the network and communications services, which was primarily run in-house, then was telco managed, and now being highly dispersed due to the advent of the Internet.

During the 1990s and early 2000s, globalization of service delivery was widespread. India-based offshore delivery centers were leveraged to remotely deliver application support, applications development, infrastructure operations and business process operations.

Today, a massive disruption is taking place in IT outsourcing. This disruption is led by the following three key factors:

- Ubiquitous availability of Internet connectivity across the globe.
- The proliferation of mobile devices in the consumer space.
- Cloud services available at scale for computing, platform services, and software services delivered from distributed cloud regions over Internet to mobile devices.

Customers are changing their IT organization structures from 'technology tower-based' to 'technology as well as business service-based'. It will bring a new approach to outsourcing. For example, the outsourcing RFPs are asking for products and platform services, DevOps services, user-experience services, operations and engineering services.

2.2 Business Case for Outsourcing

There are a few key drivers for outsourcing:

Cost Reduction

Cost reduction is one of the key driving factors for outsourcing. However, it may not be the only criteria. Outsourcers are definitely able to provide cost advantage because of the scale and the methods of operations. The motive behind cost reduction is to create funds to invest in business transformation. However, the fund that is created in the process is only sufficient for some incremental changes.

Most often, they need a radical change. Radical changes are not only expensive but difficult as well. So, the cost saving criteria may not serve the long-term purpose.

However, it will still be a key driver because it is still a good thing for the customer. That said, it will continue to lose its importance among the list of criteria.

To explain it further, it is possible to maintain service quality and still reduce the cost by virtue of automation, standardization, and volume. However, there is a threshold point up to which it would be viable. After that, a further pressure to decrease the price will result in the decline in the service quality. It is extremely important to determine that threshold point to maintain the service quality throughout at optimal price.

Bringing in Best Practices

Bringing in best practices is a valid and important criterion. It indirectly implies that the customer acknowledges that they do not have best practices. To meet the success criteria, it is important that all of the customer IT organization is aligned to the goal of bringing in best practices and quitting their existing bad practices. This could be a challenge at times because the misalignment of even one tower in the customer organization may derail the whole initiative of bringing in best practices.

Bringing best practices requires discipline, and that may pose some inconveniences. One common problem is the bureaucratic approval processes within the organization, especially for change management. Best practices demand for the optimization of approval processes, which is rarely met. The other constraint of bringing in best practices is that good things cost money; it is NOT free.

Focus on Core Competencies

This criterion was promoted by many research analysts to CXOs as a strategy to outsource trivial operations, and to free up their in-house resources that can focus on the core business.

Application-level domain expertise and Business-aligned IT architecture are typically considered as the core competency of the office of the CIO.

Need to Catch-Up with Rapidly Changing Technology

Large organizations are facing tough competition from born digital enterprises. They need to catch up fast. Born digital organizations are using cutting-edge technology, and they understand the born digital consumers well.

Outsourcing is the most attractive proposition to be agile and deal with rapid technology change by using the providers' resources who already have acquired expertise in trends and technology. Outsourcing also helps to deal with elasticity of the business because of the seasonal demand and supply.

In addition, globalization is creating the need for multilingual and 24X7 operation. Enterprises will have severe constraints on creating and maintaining skilled resources, but outsourcer can cover these constraints easily. Radical restructuring in IT achieved by outsourcing could be a positive by-product of outsourcing.

2.3 Customer's Faulty Perspective on Service Delivery

Outsourcing contracts are written while keeping the ideal state in mind, and it is not exhaustively validated during due diligence. They are more focused on 'what' and not on 'how'. There are two kinds of issues with these contracts. The first issue is around the change in requirements, and usually requires a contract amendment change.

The second issue is the bugs (anomalies) in the contract that are discovered during operations. We all understand that when an application bug is detected in production, we fix the bug, the same concept should be applied for fixing bugs in the contract.

Task-based Outsourcing vs Outcome-based Outsourcing

Typically, the error starts from the structure of Request for Proposal (RFP) and the RFP response. Clarity on vendors' roles about 'managing technology' versus 'managing end-to-end service' is often missing.

While the vendor's intent may be to go for managed service, RFP documents dictate several task-level requirements that customers want the service providers to do. Ideally, in managed-service outsourcing, the customer should specify the results to be achieved (in terms of the SLA) rather than tasks to be performed.

Moreover, these tasks are usually not well-defined and do not form the complete process. These tasks are more often listed for technology management and, thus, do not guarantee the production of the expected service and service levels. And the problem does not end here; the customer specifies both the task as well as the result—that too without any conditions. Unfortunately, tasks do not produce results; it is the process that produces the result. Therefore, if those tasks are not logically connected in a well-defined process, the desired result may not be achieved.

Managed-service providers also undertake services on an 'As-Is' process basis and the process is owned by the customer. In such a scenario, the vendor should be responsible for performing the task and producing the deliverable but not accountable for the result.

Since outsourcing service providers deliver a price advantage for executing tasks, the deal looks good on paper. However, soon these services turn out to be a 'mess for less' proposition. This is a result of mixing responsibility with accountability, or rather not differentiating them in the context of tasks and processes.

Yet, another expectation is around thought leadership. Where is the scope of thought leadership in just task outsourcing?

There are a lot of sourcing advisory and consulting companies that are paid hefty amounts by customers who seek to outsource their IT infrastructure management and application management. These consulting companies are apparently experts in guiding and managing the vendor selection process, but still fail to differentiate between technology management and service management.

In fact, they repeat the same faulty concept of dictating the tasks but expecting the result.

This tendency of committing the same mistake repeatedly reminds me of Albert Einstein's definition of insanity: "Doing the same thing over and over again and expecting a different result."

Is Security Risk & Compliance Ownership Outsourced?

The legal liability of security compliance is always with the customer. Security is strongly a matter of developing and implementing a set of control policies and procedures that are always dictated and owned by customer. Execution of those policies does not make a service provider liable for security compliance provided the service provider correctly executes those procedures and policies.

How to Deal with Outsourcing Contract Anomalies

A contractual anomaly is defined as terms and clauses that are incorrect, incomplete, contradictory or ambiguous. Here are a few examples:

- The contract-stated SLA on incident resolution: The best practice for incident resolution SLA requires the inclusion of pending time in the SLA. At times, pending tickets are in the pending state because the end-user has not taken any action. In general, the customer's interpretation does not consider the pending time in SLA measurement.

- Infrastructure service provider signs the SLA for keeping the patch level to n-n with no exception. When the provider meets these SLAs, it causes the SLA of the application service provider to break because in some cases the application breaks when the patch is applied.

- Application SLAs are higher than or equal to the server and network availability SLAs.

Service delivery based on a contract with bugs is often non-viable. Every contract has a change control clause, and every customer is expected to be committed for the success of the outsourcing model. Therefore, in such cases, it is important to have an open discussion with strong reasoning and logic.

3 The Service Delivery Manager (SDM)

The service delivery management role has different meanings in different contexts. See Figure 8 to understand it in detail.

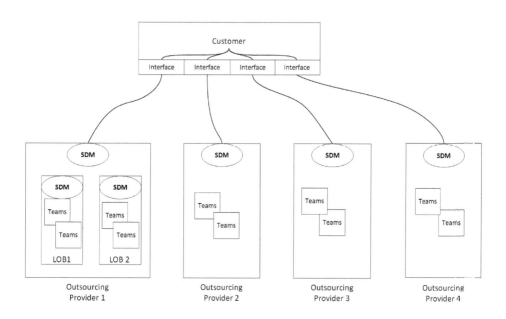

Figure 8: Meaning of Service Delivery Manager in the Context of Environment/Organization

3 THE SERVICE DELIVERY MANAGER (SDM)

Usually, the SDM is responsible for overall service delivery (and service support) to the customer from an outsourcing service provider organization.

In a multi-supplier outsourcing scenario, each service provider will have an individual SDM for all services being delivered from that service provider. Some outsourcing service providers may have internal structures separating lines of business in an integrated outsourcing service contract.

In such cases, they may structure the service delivery roles for each Line of Business (LoB). For example, an infrastructure SDM and an applications SDM. Further, a service provider may structure the delivery team based on geography and may insert geography based SDM roles such as an onsite SDM and an offshore SDM.

It is possible that some internal functions may underperform. At the end of the day, the SDM is responsible for driving all internal functions towards successful service delivery.

In the context of this edition of the book, we define an SDM as a person who directly interacts with the customer on a day-to-day basis. The future edition of this book will expand this role across LOBs and may cover the role of an in-house SDM as well.

Regardless of the size of the IT landscape in which an SDM operates, it is the most important role that helps an IT organization realize its vision.

CONTEMPORARY IT SERVICE DELIVERY IN ENTERPRISE

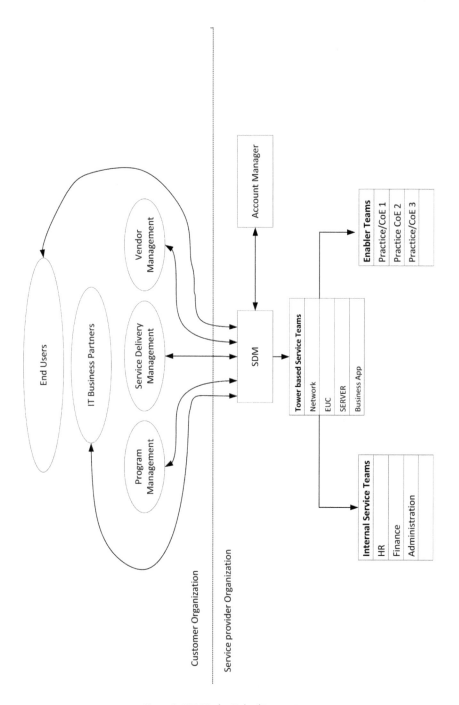

Figure 9: SDM is the Hub of Interactions

3 THE SERVICE DELIVERY MANAGER (SDM)

3.1 Typical Day in the Life of SDM

Typically, an SDM is usually expected to focus on four important activities on a daily basis.

Access to Service Management - it is imperative for an SDM to have their own account credentials in the service management system, so that they can directly access the system to review the last 24 hours tickets, randomly audit the tickets for quality and compliance. This should give them a fair amount of knowledge and insight into operational activity, and the ability to generate reports and identify operational trends.

Operational Reviews - the next important activity for an SDM is participation in daily calls at the tower/track level. Be it internal or customer calls, they should participate as a listener or as an active participant depending on the situation. It helps SDM to get a full view of what is happening in each tower, and should plan to focus on one tower every day.

Automation - another important activity for an SDM is to have regular discussions with team members to explore automation opportunities in a given space. Along with automation they can also explore the options for value creation and things which are outside of the day to day operations.

Team Management - last but not the least, an SDM should have regular skip-level meetings with the operations team to understand the soft aspects of operations. People and teams are an essential aspect of operations, and the best service delivery organizations are the ones with the lowest level of attrition. These meetings will help in grooming some of the team members and identify top performers in the team. The SDM can ignite passion, and influence the thought process by being transparent & value-centric. Finally, it is strongly recommend to have an all-hands meetings at least once in a month with the entire operations team to discuss focus areas and customer priorities.

However, in a real business environment, SDM's responsibilities are much larger and we will elaborate those in subsequent sections.

3.2 SDM: Who are You?

3.2.1 You are Defined by What You Have

Order Taker: An order taker is the one who never says 'No' to a customer. This is Level 1 in the status value chain. We consider this as the minimum requirement for an SDM.

Service Provider: A service provider will work as per the contract to meet the SLAs. This is Level 2 in the status value chain. Service provider will usually not say 'no' to any service delivery, and will have a good service-management system that incorporates best practices.

Trusted Advisor: A trusted advisor will bring customer on the right path by advising/reasoning if the customer goes wrong. The customer will listen to his 'No'. Of course, some customers may go against your advice, but nevertheless the advisor has done his job.

Strategic Partner: The customer will involve the strategic partner in their strategic decisions. The key difference between a trusted advisor and a strategic partner is that the customer will seek advice on operational matters (like how to deal with different kind of scenarios in technology operations) from the trusted advisor 'after' a strategic decision has been implemented. However, the customer will involve a strategic partner 'before' making a strategic decision.

The SDM's status value is defined by what they have as depicted in Figure 10 on the next page.

This status value will play a significant role in dealing with a customer. Higher status will automatically bring in higher level of co-operation from the customer.

3 THE SERVICE DELIVERY MANAGER (SDM)

The SDM's growth within the organization is also linked to the capability progress in customer context. However, the capability progress in the customer organization is not the only criterion for progress, the SDM needs to meet their organization's goals as well.

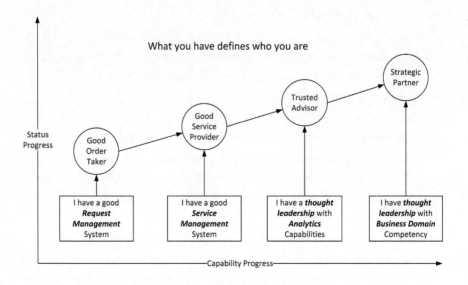

Figure 10: What You have Defines Who You are

3.3 SDM: Why are You in this Position?

Order Taker or a Good Order Taker

It is not bad to be a 'good order taker' as you are good after all. But it is definitely not good to just be an order taker. If you are in this position (first block) you do not need to be demoralized but need to strive for progress. If you are not even in the first block, then you are in trouble indeed.

In order to be a good order taker, you must register every order and track it to completion. If you do not have a good request-management system, then you are merely an order taker and not a good order taker. You will be in a crisis-management situation all the time.

In other words, a good order taker runs the operation on the foundation of a catalog and that catalog is not likely to be static. So, catalog maintenance and order tracking are the major focus areas.

Service Provider or a Good Service Provider

Being a good service provider is a tough job, yet it is satisfying. It is better to be a good order taker than to be a bad service provider. You are in this position because you have passed Level 1, but you are still learning to pass through the second test of being good for service delivery.

Just like the difference between an order taker and a good order taker, there is a difference between being a service provider and a good service provider. A good service provider will always have a good service-management setup (tools, processes, and functions), to manage the service delivery and service-support lifecycle.

Trusted Advisor has Moral Responsibilities too

You need to be the believer of a defendable point of view and righteous to be a trusted advisor. Do not expect that every advice will be adhered to, but that should not discourage you. The role of trusted advisor requires you to bring subject matter expertise to the table. If you are not an expert, then you should have a Center of Excellence (CoE) working within your organization. You need to leverage the CoE to create and maintain the cutting-edge expertise so that you can serve your customer better.

Furthermore, as you are sitting at the interface level of the CoE for your customers, you need to add value through the flow of knowledge and expertise that comes from the CoE.ws

Strategic Partner

While vertical knowledge is advantageous for a strategic partner, infrastructure service providers can secure this status in some specific technical areas by acquiring thorough knowledge of subject matter.

3.4 SDM: What is Expected from You

SDM carries a variety of responsibilities including technology management, service management, and business management among others. SDM is not only required to manage the customer's expectations, but also the expectations of the service provider.

3.4.1 General Operations

Be Good in Your Positioning

Whether you are an order take or a strategic partner, you need to faithfully justify your position and win the customer's confidence.

It will be futile to be a good order taker and attempt to position yourself as a good service provider. Similarly, it would be disadvantageous to be perceived as good order taker while you really are a good service provider.

Progress Capabilities and Status

Once your positioning baseline is well established, you need to work towards achieving the next level. That means, you need to plan and acquire the skills, knowledge, and systems for the next level.

Role	Essential Skills
Order Taker	• Ability to consistently offer professional, friendly, and engaging service. • Communication skills with etiquettes. • Knowledge of service delivery and support procedures and policies. • Knowledge of all resources available for service delivery. • Sense of responsibility.
Service Provider	• Good understanding of SLA and scope of service • Ability to maintain and improve efficient and effective service delivery system (process, tool, and functions). • Good and general-purpose understanding of all technologies • Good understanding of business alignment of all services in scope. • Sense of accountability.

3 THE SERVICE DELIVERY MANAGER (SDM)

Trusted Advisor	• Thinking and analysis. • Strong subject matter expertise. • Credibility, impartiality and integrity. • Demonstrate interests for customer benefit and show enthusiasm and connect with customer emotionally.
Strategic Partner	• Business domain expertise. • Relationship management.

Improve the Gross Margin

SDM is deemed to be a P&L owner and carries the responsibility of improving the gross margin of his account. There is constant demand for managing the margin while being the head of customer engagement.

It requires attention to all the details of costs and revenue items without compromising on day-to-day operations. Since most of the outsourcing deals are signed for three to five years, there are always changing cost elements – be it third party costs, license costs, maintenance costs, resource costs or technological changes. One needs to pay attention to every line item and find ways and means to monitor, measure, and manage the variables.

Some important points that must be understood by SDMs are:

- Business case upon which the outsourcing contract was signed.

- Savings and benefits are distributed equally across the period or lopsided with either forward or backward loading.
- When cost elements are beyond just resource cost, the customer might have preferences about how to allocate the costs in CapEx or OpEx.
- All third-party costs include the costs of software licensing, hosting services, hardware, maintenance and communications.
- Resource mix with respect to the skill level of resources, location, and the onsite/offshore spread.
- Productivity accounting as contracts typically warrant cost reduction with time, and thus requiring the provider to improve productivity.

Steady State Compliance

Compliance plays a key role in monitoring and managing the heath of operations.

If an organization wants to do business in a country with strict privacy laws, or in a heavily-regulated market such as healthcare and finance, or with a client that has high confidentiality standards, they must play by the rules and bring their security up to the required level. For example, regulations like HIPAA and SOX, or standards like PCI-DSS or ISO 27001, outline very specific security criteria that a business must meet to be deemed compliant.

A high-profile client may require the business to implement very strict security controls, even beyond what might be considered reasonably necessary in order to award their contract. These objectives are critical to success because a lack of compliance will result in a loss of customer trust, even if it is not outright illegal to conduct business in the market.

Each organization defines a set of compliance parameters to measure the health of service delivery to customers. Usually a service provider develops and maintains a suitable delivery framework aimed at conducting independent review of existing operations and propose a set of recommendations to improve the overall service-level obligations.

The primary focus is to improve customer satisfaction by ensuring that the operations team understands and acts to meet the contractual, legal, and regulatory requirements.

As a delivery head, you need to proactively maintain a checklist of service-assurance parameters against which operational compliance and stability is validated. This also benefits customers since these audits provide the necessary insight into regulatory and compliance gaps, if any.

Penalty Avoidance

Lack of awareness about contractual obligations, and not reading the statement of work thoroughly is a common mistake on the part of many SDMs. When entering into a contract, parties should be careful of clauses that seek to recover a specific monetary amount from the other party or to compulsorily acquire property of the other party, where that other party has failed to fully perform its contractual obligations.

SDM needs to proactively monitor the metrics to ensure they avoid penalties stipulated in the contract. Some of the SDMs assume that if a SLA is missed, then they can always seek exceptions from the customer.

If a provider has agreed on an SLA, the SDM or the team needs to deliver on the same. If the SLA is impractical, they need to negotiate and agree with the customer, and get the contract clauses amended. Documentation is an important aspect as verbal agreements will not hold sway if stakeholders change.

Be an Automation Champion

IT automation is defined as the use of scripts & tools to create a repeated process that replaces an IT professional's manual work in data centers and cloud environments.

Automation is no more an option. There is some scope of automation everywhere. It could be as simple as automating a notification and registering a response, and as complex as the orchestration of provisioning a complete compute environment.

IT is stuck being tactical as it continues to use tools that require much manual intervention and effort. For IT to be a differentiator, it is strategic to automate IT operations because it brings flexibility into IT operations.

Several technological changes and the evolving business world have made IT automation inevitable.

Automation with reference to IT service delivery is a journey which starts with the identification of opportunities. In the eyes of a practitioner automation can be implemented in two parts; one is basic automation using scripts and other mechanisms, and the other is complex automation using platforms to drive outcomes.

Basic automation is where the given tasks are automated using simple scripts and reducing the errors and reduction of manual efforts. In complex automation you are leveraging the platform as the foundation for all your activities. Software tools, frameworks, and appliances conduct the tasks with minimum administrator intervention.

The scope of IT automation ranges from single actions to discrete sequences, and ultimately to an autonomous IT deployment that takes actions based on user behavior and other event triggers. Mobile technologies, cloud computing, data analytics and other emerging technologies along with IT operations automation have exponentially improved the chance for business innovations to take shape and bear fruits.

It has become imperative for all delivery heads to become automation champions since they are the ones who work closely with the customer and understand their business and processes. Automation should be ingrained in the psyche of a delivery head and they should understand the tools and technology which are available to drive automation.

Based on the changing environment, you can see most of the towers will go down in terms of the number of support people but automation and process tower will see a surge in those numbers.

Value Creation & Continual Improvement

One needs to consistently create value and focus on continual improvement as IT management in involves different transactions on an ongoing basis. We need to challenge the teams on the ground to review every activity they perform and identify optimization opportunities. A simple approach in this regard is to encourage every team member to identify opportunities to save cost, save time or increase value and satisfaction.

Innovation in Operations

Innovation in operation is a bit different from value creation; it is the out-of-box thinking you need to bring to your operations and delivery. Innovation is not incremental in nature and typically drives radical and disruptive changes in IT architecture and technology.

Control Freebees in the Operation

Control does not mean stopping; it means do not make it a habit. It should be an exception. Nothing is free, so if you are giving something free, in reality you have charged for it in some way or form. If not, it is against basic business principles.

Escalate for the Right Matter

Escalation is not a bad thing. When and what to escalate is an important aspect of the SDM's role. This comes with the deep understanding of operations and criticality of the application landscape that one is managing.

No one in the management chain likes to get surprises. Providing strong recommendations, and escalating where required is a contractual obligation. One needs to pay attention to this aspect, and define all levels of escalations and triggers from one level to other level. Having a well-defined escalation matrix, and forward thinking is one of the success formulae for stakeholder management.

Conflict of Interest with Customer and Organization

SDM needs to maintain a healthy balance between the interests of their own organization and that of the customer. Since we are morally obligated to be loyal to the organization we are working for, an SDM should prioritize organizational interest while delivering services to the customer (without deviating from business code of conduct).

Servicing the customer beyond the scope of contract without additional revenue in order to keep the customer happy is a prime example of conflict of interest between the customer and delivery organization, as you are delivering something free although it costs you. Such scenarios must be controlled.

In a conflicting situation, an SDM should focus on the interests of their own organization and charge the customer for the services rendered.

Another example of conflict of interest would be sometimes customers get used to a set of resources (conflict of resource rotation), and would like to continue with the same resources who are not part of the managed service contract. Instead of having a meaningful conversation with the customer to change the type of contract and billing, we tend to continue as it is so that it does not impact our relations with the customer. As a matter of fact, we are being disloyal to our own organization by not charging for the special services we are offering. A customer appreciates honesty and transparency in a relationship rather than creating a conflicting situation.

3.4.2 Embed Service Management with Technology Management

Every enterprise landscape will include diversified technology components. There are multiple technology vendors in each area, and each vendor will provide best practices, guidance, and procedures specific to their area. You will use these manuals to manage the technology. However, there is a difference between the management of technology and management of service. You as a service provider are obligated to come out with your service-management best practices.

IT professionals deal with technology and managing technology and that will continue to be true. But technology management does not automatically mean service management, and you need as much attention on service management.

For example, I am a server administrator and I need to install a patch. On the technology side, when I am applying the patch, I must follow the best practice guide provided by the operating system vendor. However, I must also follow the change management process that will ensure that the patch is tested, risk is assessed, and that I am utilizing the permitted maintenance window. All this will come from my change management process.

Technology management and service management process need to work together as described above, and illustrated in the following diagram.

CONTEMPORARY IT SERVICE DELIVERY IN ENTERPRISE

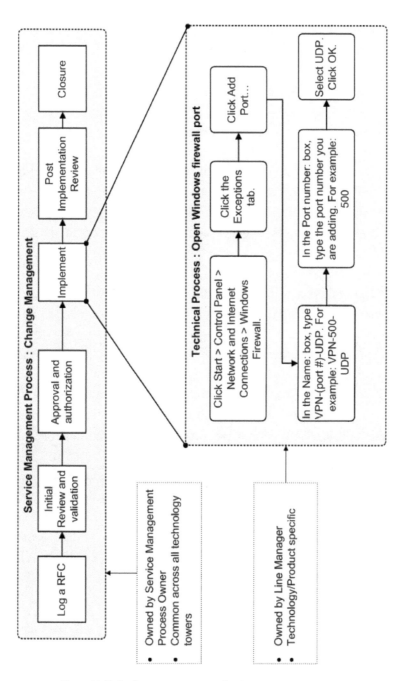

Figure 11: Technology management vs Service management process

Technology management processes rely upon service-management process to work, and vice versa. They are complementary to one another.

3.4.3 Team Management

People Management vs. Role Optimization

While leading and managing people is one aspect, role optimization is another. It deals with the completeness and right sizing of the team. A service delivery team is considered to be complete when all roles required to manage the services under a contract are mapped to designated individuals.

This requires process oriented thinking because it will change the perspective. Server Administrator is a technology management role, but how does it fit into a service-management role. It does when you map roles such as Incident Resolver, Problem Investigator, Change Implementer, and Request Fulfiller to the Server Admin. Once you do that, it would be very easy to determine the missing roles that have not been mapped to any individual, and then make the team complete by allocating those roles or adding persons to undertake missing role.

Team sizing is a matter of determining the right size based on the workload. Workload is decided by the operational pipeline of all process roles. An SDM may add many server administrators and each administrator may be mapped to a role such as Incident Resolver, Problem Investigator, Change Implementer and Request Fulfiller. Alternatively, the SDM may allocate Problem Investigator and Change Implementer role to a few Server Admins and other Server Admins could be Incident Resolvers and Request Fulfillers.

Decision Making is an Integral Responsibility

While running day-to-day business such as operations, an SDM needs to take a variety of decisions in technical and non-technical domains such as HR, personnel, administration, commercial and financial matters. It is expected that those decisions will be well-informed, but in real life there is much more beyond data-driven decisions.

The decision-making style makes a lot of difference and influences the success or failure of the decision. SDMs should learn the art and science of decision making, as well as implementing the decision in practice.

Democratic Approach

In this style, the decision-making power is distributed without any individual privileges. SDM, while deciding in a democratic manner is merely the facilitator and not exercising his managerial authority. Although democratic decisions are popular, they may not necessarily be the right or the best decisions. A democratic method is more likely to arrive at decisions driven by what people feel rather than what they know. Drastic decisions that are likely to have a strong or far-reaching effect are not taken by a democratic method. A democratic approach is suitable for the following scenarios:

1. The outcome of the decision is not critical and, therefore, has relatively high tolerance for error or implications are not risky.
2. The knowledge to take the right decision is not with an individual, and collective wisdom is required.
3. SDM is chartering into some new territory and wants to conduct some experiment. It is about a trial, analysis, and evaluation.

Pros and Cons of Democratic Decisions

Pro	Con
• Decision is highly acceptable because of the majority it is involved. • Decision creates the spirit of team involvement and togetherness as a consequence. • Minimum hurdle in implementation because majority is associated with the decision. • Low on risk of failures.	• Time-consuming process because a larger group needs to get involved—the group may be spread across different geographies and time zones. • Resource needs to coordinate and collaborate including tools and environment to conduct the decision-making process. • Lack of accountability / ownership; it is everybody, and therefore nobody. • Lack of initiative because an individual will not pursue with a vigor.

Here are the examples when SDM may want to make democratic decision.

These are usually internal to SDM's organization not in customer's area.

1. Operational policies that concern everyone such as resource allocation, shift assignment, awards and rewards.
2. Routine methods and tools of collaborations within teams.

Diplomatic Approach

Diplomacy is the skill in handling affairs without arousing hostility among the concerned people. Diplomatic decisions are successful if initiated by an empowered person, and if the right people are involved in the process.

SDM is an empowered person, and therefore the right person to initiate the diplomatic process to arrive at decision. Diplomatic method has its value when:

1. There are multiple knowledge holders and multiple point of views among stakeholders. Each stakeholder will press for the decision that they thinks is right based on their knowledge and point of view.

2. Team involvement is essential but majority is not the criteria; instead, consensus of everyone is required and that would require deliberations. Consensus is a pursued majority, and carries the benefits of an absolute majority.

Pro and Cons of Diplomatic Decision

Pro	Con
• Diplomatic method is not democratic, but it appears to be democratic and, therefore, • carries all the benefits of democracy.	• Decision can be demoralizing, if diplomacy is not used skillfully. Instead of pursued majority, it could be a forced majority that has its implications during implementation phase.

Here are some examples when an SDM may want to take a diplomatic approach. These could be internal to the SDM's organization or within customer organization.

3 THE SERVICE DELIVERY MANAGER (SDM)

1. SDM wants to adopt certain technology/tools or change the process that has an impact on customer.

2. SDM wants to make some organizational changes within the teams, and that change has an impact on delivery within and outside the customer environment.

Bureaucratic Approach

Bureaucratic decisions are desirable for large organizations and engagements. Bureaucracy results from organizational culture or individual personalities and is rooted in the psychology of fear of being blamed for wrong decisions. This fear forces the SDM to create evidence of his actions in the system, which takes time and effort.

A bureaucratic approach is suitable when:

1. Approval is required for finalization, based on organizational policy.

2. Justifications are vitally important to support the decision.

3. Outcome has audit and legal considerations after the decision has been made and the scope of such audit is open ended in timeframe.

Pro and Cons of Bureaucratic Approach

Pro	Con
• Defined rules must be followed to arrive to the decision.	• Very time consuming. • Very resource intensive.

• Decision making itself is process-driven and every step is deemed to be designed with a logic. • From the point of initiation to conclusion, the system is open and visible to all stakeholders.	

Here are the examples when SDM may want to take the bureaucratic approach. These could be internal to SDM's organization or within customer organization.

1. SDM wants to take a disciplinary action against a team member.
2. Decisions that requires compliance or legal validations.
3. SDM wants to take investment decision.
4. SDM wants to change the SLA or amend the contract that are open for interpretation.

Autocratic Approach

The Autocratic Approach can be applied when an individual has vast power and sole decision making authority. Success of autocratic decision depends upon the integrity of the individual (not promoting vested interest), and also depends upon the enforceability and judgments of the individual.

Pro and Cons of Autocratic Approach

Pro	Con
• It is swift and fast as one person alone is taking the decision. • Decision is more likely to be righteous.	• Autocratic approach is likely to suppress opportunity for individuals. • Lack of team involvement and probability of resistance in implementation.

Here are the examples when SDM may want to take the autocratic approach.

1. Service-management transformation that lead to value adds.
2. Team motivations and promotions.
3. Hiring of right and competent candidate.
4. Financial approval of expenses within budgets.

3.5 The Essential Soft Skills for SDM

In service delivery, service support, and team management, soft skills are critically important. Soft skills enable you to interact effectively and harmoniously with other people.

Soft Skills for Service Support

In a customer support situation, you need to handle the expectations and perceptions of the customer first before you address the problem. The customer has emotions that must be addressed before the technical or commercial solution is offered. This is also an opportunity to gain customer loyalty by establishing a rapport with the customer.

1. Passion: Passion to deliver excellent customer service is a very important aspect of service delivery. One should have the passion to learn, share and be trained consistently. SDM should assure the current service, and continue to build on existing best practices. She needs to be a role model for the team so there is accountability across the board.

2. Empathy: The Must-Have skill for all SDMs is to have empathy towards the customer. When a customer reaches out for service, he wants to be heard and wants you to understand the issue. Customers will have their own pressure from their top management and business users. At times they could seem unreasonable, but try and put yourself in their position and provide the best.

Customer service cannot always deliver solutions but it can always deliver empathy. One of the best techniques is to listen, understand the concerns and deliver empathetic solutions across multiple touchpoints. A successful SDM is one who is personable and shows empathy when needed and also stand firm on issues if necessary.

3. Interpersonal skills: SDM should have the ability to communicate (both verbal, written, including e-mail etiquette) and translate effectively across various customer stakeholders. Persuasion, presentation and active listening and learning are key aspects here.

If you listen to the customer patiently, the customer will have confidence in you. Never interrupt a customer and let him finish. It is equally important that the customer understands you. Use appropriate language and speak slowly and clearly. Your empathetic words will keep the interaction positive.

4. Temperament: Avoid excessive sensitiveness or irritability during the conversation. It will lead to dispute and arguments. Control your negative emotions. This will help bring the customer out of negative emotions, if any.

3 THE SERVICE DELIVERY MANAGER (SDM)

5. Probing Skill: Asking the right questions is the first step towards obtaining the right and accurate information. Ensure that you are not encroaching the confidentiality of the customer's information such as contractual terms of other service providers.

6. Negotiation Skill: Customers will often expect you to perform the best-case delivery over and above the SLA, and that may not be possible. For example, if the SLA dictates you to resolve the issue within 4 days, and the customer wants it within 2 days because of genuine reasons, then instead of finding an immediate solution, you can negotiate for a workaround.

This kind of negotiation often takes place to set the expectation level dynamically. Good negotiation skills will help you to avoid undue pressure to perform the impossible.

7. Situation Management: Customers expect us to solve problems quickly and efficiently. When a problem has a considerably high impact on the business, it becomes a situation. In order to manage a situation, an SDM should be able to mobilize resources, perform escalations, lead problem resolution team, report and communicate powerfully and conduct lessons-learned sessions.

You have the procedures and plans for most situations but how do you identify the right ones? You have many talented teams but one needs to know how to work together to produce consistent results in a complex business environment.

Some of the challenges would be to manage teams distributed across regions, shift changes and other dynamic factors. Mastering these competencies allows SDMs to solve the problems quickly and efficiently.

Telling No to the Customer

You will occasionally come across situations when you cannot fulfill the demand of the customer, and you are required to say 'no' to the customer.

Do not be nervous about saying no. However, there is a method to say no. You must use all your verbal and communication skills to explain why you are saying no to a specific demand, along with a counter offer that would likely meet the purpose of the original demand.

Please note that telling 'no' for non-viable (and free) things does not constitute bad customer service and likewise saying 'yes' for everything (right or wrong) does not constitute good customer service.

Soft Skills for Team Management

1. Teamwork: This skill will help you to combine action of all team members and make it effective and efficient towards a common goal. You can make each member deliver at their best. For example, soft skills of the service desk and technical skills of the resolution group make the perfect combination to satisfy the customer as well as fix the problem.

2. Dependability: Dependability makes you trustworthy and reliable. You should be dependable for your team and vice versa.

3. Adaptability: While customer requirements may be very dynamic, adaptability will enable to adjust to new requirements. You should be able to modify your as well as your teams' skills for a new purpose.

4. Conflict Resolution: Conflicts of interest occur regularly at all levels, be it personal-level, team-level or customer-level. It could be as trivial as a conflict of two important meeting schedules or as critical as the conflict of personalities in your team. Conflict resolution may not be easy but you should know the technique for resolving conflicts.

Flexibility: Willingness to change or compromise will help you resolve conflicts and be adaptable. Flexibility may not be always good in service delivery processes because it may impact your standardization and automation goals. In general, you should always play by rules but define the point where you can be flexible.

3.6 *Human Failure: Errors and Violations*

Instances of failure caused by human action is human failure, and could be intentional or unintentional. Human failure can happen in technology as well as operations domain and can happen across all levels of the team (most junior to most senior).

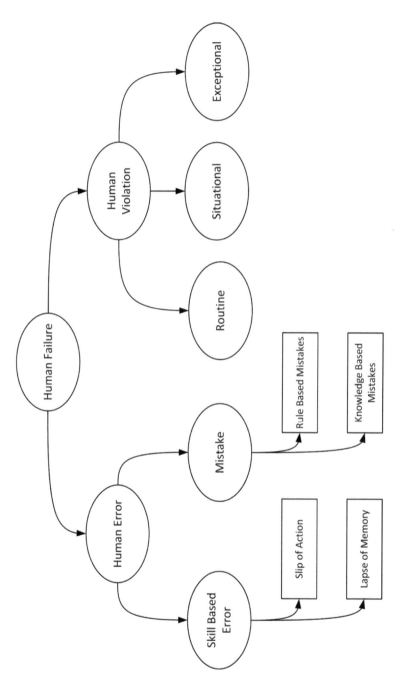

Figure 12: Human Failure

Examples of Human errors and Violations

3.6.1 Understanding and Avoiding Human Error

Skill-based errors (slips and lapses) and mistakes are two types of human errors. These can be committed by even the experienced and trained person.

Slips indicate not doing what is expected from a person while a lapse is forgetting to do something, or losing track midway through a process.

Slips and lapses can occur in day-to-day tasks which a person is well accustomed with, for example, selecting a server group while applying group policies. These kinds of tasks are very vulnerable to slips and lapses when a person's concentration is diverted even for a moment. It is a matter of a click on a screen.

Examples of slips and lapses include:
- Skipped a task in the procedure or performed incomplete task. Performed a task but incorrectly.
- Performed an extra task in the procedure that was not required for that scenario (rebooting, for example).
- Performed task in a wrong sequence.
- Performed the task at the wrong time.
- Forgot to take backups before the upgrade.
- Logged on to another server when interrupted for an urgent incident and forgot to log o and continued previous task.

Why Slips and Lapses Occur?
Slips and lapses occur when:

- Tendency to be careless when the task is very familiar and requires little thinking.
- Person gets confused with two similar tasks.
- Person has distractions and interruptions.

- Tasks are too complicated, and the execution time is long and the response on screen is slow.
- The main part is done but the finer details are missed.
- Steps in a procedure are not well designed for natural and procedural thinking.

How to Minimize Slips and Lapses?

It is important to note that, adding more training will not eliminate slips and lapses. Effective procedures are required. SDM should:

- Make all team members aware that slips and lapses do happen, and it is realistic to minimize them rather than eliminate altogether.
- Develop and implement checklists to help confirm that all actions have been completed.
- Make sure checks are in place for complicated tasks.
- Provide the working environment that is free from distractions and interruptions.

Mistakes

Mistakes are decision-making failures. They arise when a person does the wrong thing, believing it to be right such as:

- Making a poor judgement on risk assessment, and change windows when implementing a major RFC.
- An operator misinterpreting the event log in the alarm and ignoring the imminent failure.

Why Do Mistakes Occur?

1. Doing too many things at the same time; many complex tasks at once.

2. Multitasking is a faulty concept. May be tolerable while multitasking trivial activities but during important work, which requires your focus, multitasking could be dangerous.
3. Time pressure.
4. Non-conducive work environment.
5. Extreme task demands such as high workloads, boring tasks, repetitive activities, and jobs that require a lot of concentration.
6. Social issues such as peer pressure, conflicting attitudes to health and safety, conflicting attitudes of workers on how to complete work and too few workers among others.
7. Individual stressors such as drugs and alcohol, lack of sleep, family problems, ill health and such.
8. Equipment problems such as inaccurate or confusing instructions and procedures among others.
9. Organizational issues such as failing to understand where mistakes can occur and implement controls, such as training and monitoring to name a few.

How You Can Reduce Mistakes:

- To avoid rule-based mistakes (lack of policy), increase worker situational awareness of high-risk tasks, and provide procedures for predictable non-routine, high-risk tasks. There will be lot many use cases for this in Change Management Process.
- To avoid knowledge-based mistakes (lack of guidance), ensure proper supervision for inexperienced workers and provide well-maintained SOPs, manuals and knowledgebase.

3.6.2 Understanding and Avoiding Human Violations

Violations are intentional failures *(chalta hai attitude)* – deliberately doing the wrong thing. The violation of rules or procedures is one of the biggest causes of service outages. Typical violations include:

- Not performing risk assessment for critical changes.
- Person overriding the prescribed procedure with his own version of procedure.
- Assigning untrained person for a critical role (Critical Incident Manager for example).
- Assigning a person to the role without a proper induction program.

Why human violation occurs?

- Person thinks the rules do not apply to their role.
- Person is under time pressure.
- Person does not have the right tools.
- Person did not understand the technical or service management process.
- Person carries a perception that rules are too strict or unnecessary.
- Person wants to take the easy option; and that no one would detect the violation.
- Peer pressure.

How you can reduce violations:

- Implement auditing and monitoring mechanisms.
- Make sure the rules and procedures are relevant and practical.
- Explain to team the reasons behind any rules and procedures and their relevance.
- Involve teams in changes to processes to increase their acceptance.
- Improve the working environment.
- Improve planning for all jobs to ensure the necessary tools.
- Encourage the reporting of any problems (such as job pressures) through open communication.
- Provide training for abnormal and emergency situations.
- Always think about the possibility of violations when carrying out risk assessments.

3.6.3 The Doer & Checker Process

The basic concept of Doer and Checker is that the former does a step/task in the process and the latter verifies that the task was done, and whether or not it was done correctly.

Lufthansa Airlines once ran a series of the advertisement to assure the safety of travelers. The headline in that advertisement was: "We have people who check people who check people who check our aircrafts." This was an acute implementation of the doer and checker process where the airline claimed to implement the check on the checker.

The doer and checker process is one of the methods to minimize human failure, and it costs money. However, there are many use cases at least in critical and high-risk change implementation process where it could be worthwhile to invest in this approach.

3.7 Contract Renewals

Why renewal is critical? The cost and cycle time for winning a contract through an RFP is multifold to the cost and cycle time for renewing a contract. Renewing is also an opportunity to resolve the issues of the old contract such as:
1. Remove the faulty clauses of the old contract.
2. Expansion and fine tuning the scope of work.
3. Modernizing the engagement model.
4. Expectation setting of the customers, especially when the stakeholders have changed.

Typically, the preparation for renewal should start 12-18 months before the expiry of the existing contract.

Contracts are the main source of driving revenue, so why would a business risk by creating a contract with errors, delays, or worse missing a contract renewal?

To help prevent revenue leakage create a checklist for contract renewals and a faster, more accurate way to drive renewals:

Set reminders long before the start of a renewal period.
During renewal reviews, consider what was changed in the last review.
Forward the contract and related documents to the key stakeholders and internal departments.

In renewals, offering discount is an easy option, but the SDM's focus during the renewal process should be on offering a bundled deal inclusive of business focused SLAs, next-gen services and value add components.

Sense where the customer is spending their money and channelize your discussions in such a manner that it becomes a win-win deal for both you and your customer. If you look at all your customers from their spend perspective, you might be delivering only 5-10% of the total value, the remaining 90% of their budget is either going to a third party or directly to OEMs. So, the opportunity to expand your footprint is very high.

3.8 Role of SDM in Transition

SDM has an active role in the transition to avoid the common pitfalls as listed below. She works closely with the transition manager during the transition period. A transition manager walks out on the completion of the transition, but the SDM continues to ensure smooth steady state operations.

1. Context – the operation that SDM will be responsible for in 'steady state' should be based on the future ways of working rather than current ways of working. This will shift the focus from creating runbooks to

the operations manual. This requires perusing and understanding the contract and SOW ahead of time before kicking off the transition.
2. Build relationship with customer before steady state delivery commences, by interacting with the customer during transition.
3. Utilize the transition time to develop and on-board resources in time for the parallel run.
4. Ensure that some of the deliverables that were hitherto nonexistent, such as Day 1 reporting are established.
5. Expectation setting about operation and transformation deliverables.

Transition Manager and SDM during Transition

Transition Manager	SDM
• Project initiation • Project governance • Risk register maintenance • Interfacing with enablement organization • Transition tracking and reporting.	• Process Transition SME • Steady-state resource building and on boarding • Customer expectation setting • Checklist of capability for all steady-state deliverables • Including Day 1 deliverables Development of the operation manual.

Figure 13 depicts the involvement of these two roles beginning from the signing of the service contract with customer.

While transition manager's preparation starts by organizing the resources for transition, the SDM prepares by studying the contracts, SLAs, and obligations that he/she would eventually undertake.

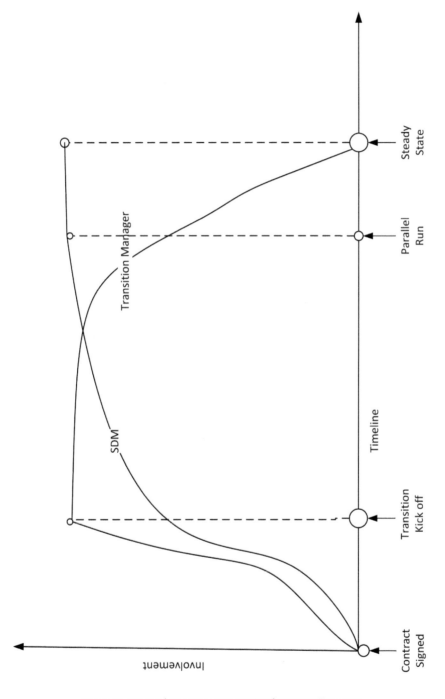

Figure 13: SDM and Transition Manager Involvement in Transition

3 THE SERVICE DELIVERY MANAGER (SDM)

Pitfalls of Transition: Process Transition Ignored

What is Process Transition?

Process Transition is required for the service provider in those engagements where the customers want the service provider to manage their infrastructure using the processes that are defined and owned by the customers. The most important goals of this Process Transition are:

a) To establish a method of transitioning the processes to service provider from a customer organization, thereby avoiding any ad-hoc approaches for undertaking service delivery.

b) To detect, highlight, and agree upon the usual lack of completeness in the customer processes to cover those aspects of service delivery, which the customers expect the service provider to perform, but their processes are unclear or insufficient to deliver such outcomes.

c) To identify the need to elaborate any aspects of customer processes and obtain procedure-level clarity before taking the ownership of executing the tasks and transactions on behalf of the customers. This is to avoid the risk of adopting insufficiently detailed processes, which may cause inconsistent delivery, business escalations or rework.

d) To ensure that right and justified measurements methods are used to measure operations after Process Transition and that the tools and reports that indicate the service provider's performance against agreed service levels are methodically correct.

A process transition will lead to process re-engineering and corrections within processes that are inadequate or not correctly designed.

Why it is Critical?

Process transition is the only opportunity to analyze and correct existing process issues. It mitigates the possibility of inheriting faulty processes and failure in steady state. Most common faults in the customers' processes are:

1. Processes are not designed for outsourcing services.
2. Processes are not designed to capture data points that are essential to measure SLAs in contract.
3. Processes are not formally established, and are ineffective and inefficient.

SDM and the Process Transition SME

SDM is the person responsible for overall service, and service-management processes are common across all services. Therefore, it is a no brainer to conclude that the SDM should be an integral part of process transition and work very closely with the SME for service management process transition.

Transformation During Transition

Customers while outsourcing service delivery and support, will often ask the service provider to bring in their own processes and tools. It is a green field situation and the service provider should take this as a process and tools transformation opportunity.

In other words, it would be cross-functional process and tool transformation during the overall transition timeline. Transition and transformation should never be mixed up and should be managed using specific methodology.

3.9 IT Service Quality Gaps

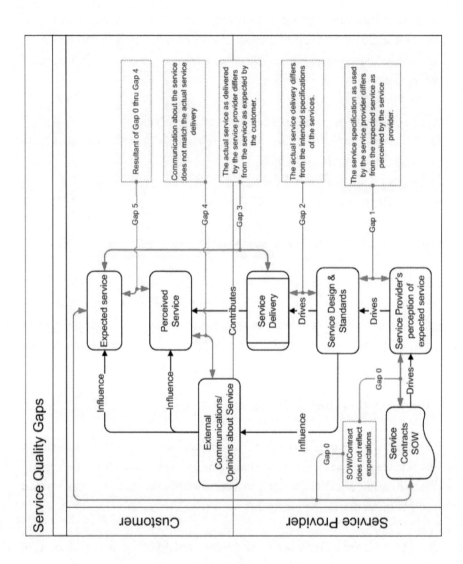

Figure 14: Service Quality Gaps

Gap 0 – gaps really start with the contractual Statement of Work (SOW) at the foundation as they usually do not reflect the expectations of the customer or provide objective parameters to the service provider. Since the SOW drives the service provider's perception of expected service, deficiency on the SOW on the expected service sets the foundation for further gaps.

Many times, the service provider prepares to deliver extraordinary things and delivers them 'ordinarily,' and the customer is still not excited because the end result is ordinary. Service providers may miss the point that the customer is expecting ordinary things but 'extraordinary' delivery.

For instance, SOW describes the implementation of a financial-management process for IT service. While the service provider thought of implementing cost models and a robust charge-back system, the customer was expecting 'timely submission of error-free invoices' as the outcome. SOWs are focused on contract arbitration rather than relationship-building, and this is one of the key weaknesses which needs to be addressed from the outset. An important point to note here is that the customer is an equal partner in setting the foundation for this gap. This is referred as Gap 0 in Figure 14.

Gap 1 – once the SOW is finalized, the service provider is required to define standards and erects service delivery systems (people, process, and tools, etc.) based on those standards. Many times however, pre-existing standards are used and the SOW requirements are not taken into account resulting in a gap.

The customer thinks that the standards to design the service are based on the SOW, and that the provider will deliver the expected service, but the standards and design may not be adequate. The service specification as used by the service provider differs from the service expected and perceived by the customer. This is referred to as Gap 1 in Figure 14.

Gap 2 – gaps arising from the theoretical definition of standards, and best practices and the actual implementation are referred to as delivery gaps. There is always a difference between what you intend to do and what you actually do, primarily because of imperfections in tools and inadequacy of training people.

For example, a customer was expecting 99.9% availability of service, but the system was not designed to serve that purpose, or if the customer was expecting the issue to be resolved at the first call, but the service desk agent was not trained in the technology needed to resolve the issue. This is referred to as Gap 2 in Figure 14.

Gap 3 – Even if everything went right till this point, the actual service delivered by the service provider may differ from the service expected by the user. The contract or SOW may not have any bearing on expectations. For example, say the SLA was three days to install the software; you designed your system and trained people to complete the installation in three days, but the customer was expecting installation in two days. This is an example of Gap 3, as shown in Figure 14. If the service provider does not do anything to set the customer's expectation, the expectation will be set by the customer.

Gap 4 – Before, during, and after service rendering, there is a regular communication between the service provider and the service receiver. Most often, these are overstated, and all claims about the capabilities and feedback do not match with actual service delivery. There are also external communications that are not usually authorized communications about the services. For example, the marketing campaign of competitors against the service provider. These communications influence the perception of the customer as well. In many cases, service providers alter their designs to align with market trends. All these factors produce Gap 4 (see Figure 14).

Service involves interaction and exchange between two parties, the service receiver and the service provider. Therefore, the service quality should be solely influenced by the actions and exchanges between these two parties.

However, in service quality gaps you will notice the influence of third parties that have no business in the service transactions also impacts the service quality and introduces gaps. This influence is because of direct and indirect communication about services that sets the customer's expectations. For example, let's suppose you have heard great things about a long-distance telephone service provider from your friend and opted for it. You were not satisfied because your expectations were set by your friend, who was not an authorized promise-maker for the provider. The brand value of the provider also provokes consumer expectations.

The resultant sum of all these issues is Gap 5 (as shown in the diagram above) and that gap stems from false perceptions and expectations combined. Both perceptions and expectations are very difficult to measure and thus make perfection in the service industry seemingly impossible.

Processes to Close the Gaps

Gap 0 is the foundation of all the gaps, even though Gap 5 is the result of all gaps and occurs because of one of the most intangible factors for measurement; Perception.

Preparation of SOW and contracts is usually dominated by legal professionals who are not the actual users or providers of services, and if stronger participation does not come from the service provider and consumer, there will always be a risk of setting the foundation for future gaps. Since customers drive SOWs and contracts, they unknowingly set up the foundation for service-quality gaps.

By translating customer-service expectations into clear service agreements, Gap 1 can be closed. In ITSM process terminology, you will need strong service-design processes, especially service-catalog management, service-level management, capacity management and availability management.

Once a comprehensive service agreement is in place, proceed towards using that agreement as a basis for planning and implementing service delivery solutions. In an ITIL context, this is the service transition lifecycle which includes service asset and configuration management, service validation, testing and evaluation.

Next, ensure that service delivery and support is done according to plans and procedures. These plans and procedures are covered in the ITIL service operation process lifecycle.

Finally, manage the configuration about service delivery via a governance process to close Gap 4. These processes are included in the service strategy and the Continual Service Improvement Process (CSIP) of ITIL.

Complexity Because of Intangibility

Perception of the service becomes very critical because of the intangibility of the service. Services are not always what they seem to be, and what they seem to be is the perception. Since the sum of service-quality gaps converges on perception, it becomes an extremely important aspect of service management. There is very little guidance available on this (maybe because ITSM is dominated by technology).

Perception management is used with positive or negative ethics. It is prominent everywhere, from marketing campaigns to diplomacy. When associated with negative ethics, it can also be called propaganda, and then it focuses on concealing the truth from the general view to gain benefits by distorting perceptions of reality. An average person is usually compliant and submissive rather than being critical, and this allows the masquerading of sub-par and bad service delivery in the guise of acceptable and good quality service.

However, perception management has positive ethics also. The service provider must prominently expose and project the positive aspects of service quality very actively to create a positive perception. If not, the default perception is likely to be disadvantageous to the service provider.

Managing Customer Satisfaction by Managing Perception

While the IT industry is leading in developing new products and services, it is seriously lagging in terms of customer satisfaction. In other industries, the focus has steadily shifted from product to customer satisfaction, and these efforts are visible in advertisements, publications, and practices.

Fortunately, the IT industry has realized, at least lately, the importance of perception management, and IT service management that focuses on this subject has started evolving. It is indeed realistic and possible to achieve higher customer satisfaction by working on customer expectations and perceptions of service quality.

This approach takes advantage of the fact that a customer is more readily prepared to criticize bad service than to appreciate good service. This realization is gaining ground. This shift in focus is justified, because customer dissatisfaction produced by not meeting basic needs is more harmful than not meeting SLAs.

However, for full satisfaction, it is very important to focus on customer expectations as well. Perception management involves continuously testing performance against customer expectations and needs, without

3 THE SERVICE DELIVERY MANAGER (SDM)

any formal agreement. This process is based on the measurement of performance and perception, and can dynamically calibrate customer expectations.

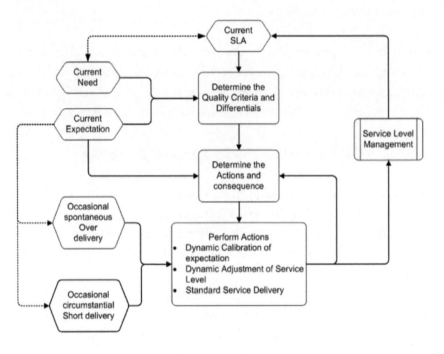

Figure 15: Perception Management

While the above diagram is self-explanatory, it is important to understand that success requires the customer and the provider to have a stronger bond than traditional partnership.

Prerequisites are as follows:

1. The customer and service provider should have a sense of respect and equality. An attempt to dominate will ensures failure.
2. Understanding each other's point of view is very important.
3. Collaboration culture should prevail with all the parties involved.

3 THE SERVICE DELIVERY MANAGER (SDM)

Take a real-life example of one of the quality criteria of 'timeliness' of service: A user reports some printer issue and is unable to print a report.

The SLA for resolution of such an incident could be eight hours, but the customer's need is four hours because she is unable to submit a report. The expectations of the user may be two hours because of external factors. So, we have three different resolution time targets – SLA of eight hours, need of four hours, and expectation of two hours. Following are the possible scenarios:

1. You are targeting the SLA. You resolved the issue in eight hours. You met the SLA, but you did not meet the expectation, nor did you meet the current need.

    a. This will result in customer dissatisfaction and a negative image of non-performance.

    b. This will place you in a disadvantageous position for future transactions of service support.

2. At a service desk, you are aware of the customer's needs and SLA, and you can evaluate the impact of not meeting the need. You decide for over delivery on this occasion. You resolve the issue in four hours even though the SLA for resolution is eight hours. You meet the need and SLA but not the expectations.

3. This is may result in customer dissatisfaction but will not place you in a disadvantageous position for future service support.

4. After understanding the expectations, and knowing the need and the SLA as well, you will most probably dynamically negotiate and recalibrate the expectation to what you can deliver. Say you reset the expectations to four hours, and you decide for over delivery on this occasion and resolve the issue in less than four hours, this will result in

customer satisfaction, and may give you an advantage in future service support transactions.

Important point to note here is that despite over-delivering with respect to SLA in the second scenario, you are still carrying the risk of customer dissatisfaction.

Guidelines for Over Delivery

Each part of a contract usually carries some standards, SLAs and contractual obligations for the service provider. Under delivery will not be acceptable to the customer, and over delivery will not be viable for the service provider as higher service standards and service levels demand additional resources and are an expensive affair.

If you over deliver, you should ensure that this over delivery is occasional only, and does not become a routine practice. Also, you must ensure that customers are cognizant of over delivery with respect to SLA or sometimes with respect to the need. You should definitely not fall in the trap of over delivery with respect to unrealistic expectations.

Apart from an economic disadvantage (that you are leaking possible revenue of higher service levels), over delivery also sets the expectations of the customer for higher service levels that is not sustainable. Whenever you decide to over deliver, make it loud and clear to the customer that it was an exception, so that future expectations are rightly set.

Under-delivering occasionally while managing customer expectation will not hurt you, as long as you meet the need. In the above example, if the customer's need was 12 hours, both the SLA and the customer's expectation was eight hours, and you resolved the issue in 10 hours after negotiating with the customer, you have still breached the SLA. However, you will still achieve customer satisfaction for that transaction, but if you do this routinely, you will have a dissatisfied customer.

3.9.1 Other Factors that Impact Service Quality

Improvements in automation and service orchestration has meant that an increasing number of services are being delivered (fulfilled) without human intervention. Consumers are empowered with self-service capabilities and automated solutions which eliminates the need for human interaction.

For instance, airlines are quite advanced in this area. Passenger check is largely handled by machines and the passengers themselves. Similarly, in banks, consumers themselves transfer money or perform several account-management services. In the IT industry, new service models such as Infrastructure as a Service (IaaS), Platform as a Service (PaaS), and Software as a Service (SaaS) are fully delivered by machines.

However, there is a potential downside to these advancements. Although service providers strive to make things intuitive and user friendly, there is a limit to the extent a machine can understand the degree of naïveté (or sophistication) of individual consumers, and accordingly recalibrate the system in real time.

Therefore, the caliber of the service consumer will also be a factor which determines the quality of service. For example, an expert user will be able to obtain more value from an automated system that is producing a service rather than an average user, who will draw less service from the same system. The limit is not the service-delivery

capability or the appetite to consume the service, but the ability to obtain the value from this kind of delivery.

3.10 SLO - The Early Operations Period

In most outsourcing deals, SLAs form part of the contract and bind entities legally. An SLO (Service-Level Objective) is another term used in lieu for a a SLA when the service provider is not willing or unable to accept the contractual obligation or penalties, but accepts and agrees to the targets.

It is also quite common in traditional IT outsourcing deals, to start the engagement with an SLO for a few months, before the SLAs kick in. This is usually done to allow the service provider to get a handle on the environment and increase their knowledge of the business applications, which in all likelihood is a pre-requisite for them to achieve the SLAs. You can consider the SLO period as a practice run where you are chartering into new or untested waters.

4 SERVICE OPERATIONS

Service Operations is the outcome of People (Functions), Process and Technology (Tools). This basic concept can be understood with the analogy of a car that takes a passenger to their destination.

Customer is the passenger, car is the process, tool is the engine powering the car, and you are the driver. You need to maintain the car (process maintenance) and manage every trip (transaction/ticket).

If you are bringing your own car, then you must maintain the car as well. If a customer is providing the car and that car is not well maintained, then you will not be able to take the customer to the destination in time and/or with comfort.

Also, if you have an untrained driver, it not only delays your own trip but also causes chaos in traffic and affects the movement of other drivers.

4.1 Process

Business and manufacturing industries long back realized that business processes and manufacturing processes are the keys to error-free performances, rather than people or technology. The same hypothesis can be expanded to state that service-management processes are the keys to error-free IT service delivery.

However, the IT industry is not yet fully convinced of this, and most IT organizations are still attempting to solve process problems with tools.

Although ITIL through their process-driven approach, made that attempt, the obvious is often not very easy to see (rather, people do not want to see it), despite realizing that most service problems cannot be corrected by technology configurations.

The job of IT operation management should be to develop standardized processes and procedures that can be used across all technology and service towers. However, this rarely happens and people are left to work with disparate processes and in technology siloes, resulting in chaotic operations.

When a crisis occurs, everyone works hard and eventually solve the crisis. If the processes were right, the problem which resulted in the crisis could have been prevented in the first place.

While quality is about delivering the service right every time, processes go a step beyond that and deliver the right level of service every time. IT organizations can no longer survive by pouring in more people and technology to improve the quality and overcome competition. They need to prioritize and optimize service-management processes.

Two common mistakes associated with process implementation are described below:

1. Tool implementation is regarded as processes implementation. This myth is a result of vendors' propagating that out-of-the-box tools implementation results in best practice.
2. Even where tools are used to automate processes, the process is still amateur. By automating bad processes, we only ensure that a bad job is done more quickly and with less effort.

Upon reading this book, we hope the reader will gain a detailed and logical explanation surrounding the benefits of a process-led approach to managing services.

4.1.1 Process Thinking

Focusing on the Customer

Every process has a primary goal linked directly or indirectly to a specific customer purpose. A process-led approach leads to customer focus.

For example, the goal of the incident management process is to restore services as soon as possible – a direct customer requirement. The goal of problem management is to identify and eliminate weaknesses in the IT landscape – although indirect, a significant contributor towards customer purpose of better availability and reliability.

Ability to Predict and Control

A well-designed process defines internal and external inputs and outputs. Logical workflow acts as an algorithm of the process that can be extrapolated to predict the next step and control the outcome. For example, in a well-designed capacity management process, you can predict seasonal demand and control the consumption of services.

Improves the Utilization of Available Resources

Process consumes resources, and resource optimization is one of the key design criteria. Continual process improvement and streamlining also addresses resource optimization. For instance, a well-defined batch job management process will significantly improve the capacity utilization of computing resources.

4 SERVICE OPERATIONS

Error Prevention

Highly mature processes make service production a matter of procedural task execution. Work instructions within processes makes the outcome predictable and consistent. Mature processes are, by design, repeatable, and repeatability of proven processes prevents errors.

Provides a View on Error Occurrence and Correction

In a complete process, there is a built-in tracking mechanism of tasks and actors, along with control mechanisms. This enables error identification and correction.

Provides Complete Measurement of the System

Processes generate a variety of data for internal as well as external consumption. These data points are fed into measurement systems.

Processes are the most critical instruments for service governance: Governance is about the right people making the right decisions, and process measurements greatly facilitate that. They allow you to make decisions based on what you know rather than what you think.

Helps Control Entropy within the IT Organization

Policies and guidelines surrounding the process are built-in controls to control entropy or disorder (entropy refers to the degree of disorder in a service management environment).

Managing Relationships between Groups

A process defines the task input and output exchange points, establishing protocol between the actors, who are usually spread across different departments or different organizations. These protocols eliminate disputes and enables service delivery actors to work towards common goals.

4.1.2 Process Thinking

If IT is deemed to be a business, then it ought to be process-driven. A process-driven organization will bring in radical change in the thinking and approach toward problem-solving and conducting business.

Employees Making Mistakes vs. Process Allowing Mistakes

The general approach is to establish a robust and proven process, and govern it continually through a process-management function. Once a process is established, identify the actor roles and assign them to appropriate resources.

It is assumed that role-players will be adequately trained as part of process implementation. The onus of producing the result is shifted onto the process, and in case of deviation from the expected result, the first check should be against the process rather than individual role players.

For example, an incident in which a change-management process implementer performed a change assigned to him, without any approval. What was the problem? The change was deemed "standard," which does not require any approval as per policy – but it was not really a standard change.

Thus, there are two problems – first, there was no validation that the RFC was really a "standard RFC" at the time of submission; and second, there was no verification at the time of assignment. The checks were made at the time of completion, which is less logical, as the error had already occurred.

The wrong approach here is that checks were applied for error detection rather than error prevention. Therefore, the question is: "Whether the issue lies with the process or with the employee"?

Employees Doing the Job vs. Employees Using Process to do the Job

In many jobs, the Key Responsibility Areas (KRAs) and goals are defined for individuals, but those KRAs are not suitable for process roles. Also, while implementing the process, role-mapping is not done appropriately.

This creates silos where individuals perform discreet tasks without the context of the whole process. In a perfect world of mature processes, it would be okay; however, in real life, process relies on the appropriate use of guidelines, and, if those guidelines are used without the adequate context, the process will fail.

For example, within the incident management process, ticket life-cycle management is the responsibility of the service-desk agent, but that does not mean that the service-desk agent is responsible for producing the solution. If this responsibility is not adequately understood, then the agent will be under pressure to produce a resolution that may not be correct. So, the employees not only need to understand their role but must also know how their role fits into the overall process.

Measuring Individuals vs. Measuring Processes

We measure the efficiency and effectiveness of the process by measuring the outcome and deliverables of the process.

For instance, when considering the incident management process, there is a comparatively more value in measuring how much time it took to fix a service disruption, as opposed to measuring how many tickets an individual resolved.

Motivating People vs. Removing Barriers

In the process paradigm, we have observed that failure to produce results are typically caused by barriers in process execution as opposed to low-morale or lack of capabilities on part of the employee.

For example, in a service desk, there is a high volume of tickets, and backlog is increasing. There are two possible options. You motivate the agents to work harder and take more tickets, or you eliminate the cause of the backlog - such as performance of tools, recurring incidents, and availability of knowledge base – thus addressing the core of the issue.

Who Committed the Error vs. What Allowed the Error to Occur?

In case of an error, the first check should always be focused on process policies, guidelines, and tasks. It is quite possible that an operation encounters certain business situations for which the existing process was not originally designed.

For example, an incident-management process is designed to receive the request to fix a break in the system and provide resolution. In this process, the request will be received, assigned, and after repair work, the incident will be resolved. What if a request is received for privileged access and handled through the same process?

4.1.3 Process Maintenance

Processes are similar to software and require maintenance. We all know and understand the importance of software-application maintenance and are willing to pay for it. However, not long ago, when the concept of software as a tangible asset was evolving, the concept of software maintenance was missing. Maintenance was typically associated with "wear and tear" and largely applicable to hardware. Now software maintenance is a well-established discipline, and its cost is accounted for.

The following attributes clarify the analogy between process and software. Both processes and software:

1. Need ongoing maintenance
2. Should be upgraded with business needs
3. Can have bugs that must be removed when detected
4. Need training for users to utilize the full potential
5. Must be compatible with other interfacing processes

A common perception of software maintenance is that it merely involves fixing bugs. However, studies and surveys over the years have indicated that the majority (over 80%) of maintenance effort is used for non-corrective actions. This perception is created by faulty processes in the organizations where users submit problem tickets for functionality enhancement demands.

The complete scope of software maintenance is the modification of a software product after delivery to correct faults, improve performance, or add functionality and attributes.

Building on the analogue, process improvements and enhancements encompass a large part of process maintenance, as opposed to fixing bugs. Process maintenance can be categorized into the following four classes:

1. Adaptive Maintenance - Dealing with changes and adapting to it in the environment.
2. Perfective - Accommodating a new or changed user requirements that concern functional enhancements to process.
3. Corrective - Dealing with errors found and fixing them.
4. Preventive - Activities aiming to increase process maturity and prevention of problems in the future.

Since the concept of process maintenance is rarely understood and practiced, there is a vacuum in this area. However, the irony of process-maintenance is that people do not pay for process maintenance, but for maintenance of tools that rarely break.

4.1.4 Why Processes Fail?

Processes are not Maintained as per Business Needs

The changing dynamics and evolution of business dictates changes in IT service delivery and support, which in turn demands process changes. Regulatory requirements also impact the process. Processes are bound to be ineffective and prone to failure unless they can stay relevant to business and compliance requirements.

A simple example is modification to the approval flow within the request fulfillment process. The organization may request for and authorize modifications to the approval flow but an amendment on paper does not mean that the process has been amended.

How was the process designed and implemented? Is the modification applicable to all requests or only to specific requests? If the approval process was automated, how easy or difficult would this modification be?

These are the design considerations that will have a bearing on the feasibility of implementing the modification.

Advice – for easy process maintenance and reconfiguration for changing business needs, ensure that the process is structured and modular, with an adequate number of sub processes and clear segregation of tasks.

Management is not Committed

The management's intent cannot be addressed in design, but management's responsibility can be built into process control.

Maturity assessments are one of the key tools which can "measure" the management's intent. There are several parameters which indicate the management's seriousness about the health of the process.

These include adequate budgeting, allocation of resources, provisioning of required tools, investment in best practices and the adoption of a good value system.

People should be recognized not only for achieving the desired results, but also for the method they have utilized for achieving those results. For example, in a right value system, a service delivery manager will be appreciated for handling a critical incident successfully, but simultaneously he will also be questioned for not preventing the critical incident.

Advice - during design, ensure that you have management's sponsorship and commitment.

Lack of Process Awareness and Understanding

Lack of process awareness amongst the support staff results in process deviations, non-compliance and failures. This could be due to lack of process documentation, absence of process training or the complicated nature of the process itself.

One common theme of misunderstanding is about the guidelines in the process. Most of the time, guidelines look good on paper but are not meaningful in implementation, because they are very generic and open to interpretation. Ambiguity of guidelines is the source of errors and inconsistencies.

Advice – design intuitive and customer specific processes, and ensure that the staff is formally trained and tested at periodic intervals.

The Process is Tedious or Ineffective

Tediousness does not just mean laborious, but it is also associated with boredom. Anything that is not interesting and requires effort will be done with more errors and makes the process ineffective.

For instance, in order to perform change risk assessment, a lot of information must be keyed into the RFC that is already available in other systems. If we are unable to import that information, the task will be tedious and automatically becomes error-prone.

Tediousness usually stems from navigational or performance issues with tools. Paper-based or manual processes can also make tasks tedious due to lack of automation. For example, filling out an MS Word form and then sending it as an attachment over e-mail.

Advice – design efficient, agile and streamlined processes. Leverage automation, and eliminate redundant and bureaucratic tasks.

Participants are not Properly Trained

Training is often ignored. In fact, most people treat many process tasks as a matter of common sense. The problem is not the absence of common sense but the variation in the common sense of individuals. Training is required to bring in consistency with respect to interpretation of guidelines and decision making.

Advice – design intuitive and customer specific processes, and ensure that the staff is formally trained and tested at periodic intervals.

Insufficient Tools to Follow the Processes

Thomas Carlyle, a famous Scottish satirical writer, once said, "Man is a tool-using animal. Nowhere do you find him without tools; without tools he is nothing, with tools he is all." Yes, he is right, and this is true for people in the field of IT. Tools make life easy. If something can be easily done with a tool, then make that tool available.

Advice - the need for tools should be primarily addressed during implementation. The process should be designed to leverage the capabilities of the tools which are at your disposal.

Time Constraints

You must allow realistic amount of time to execute tasks in the process, while providing alternate process models to handle emergencies.

For example, all IT organizations have an emergency change-management process where you bypass some regular tasks but not every task. You still have controls for emergency. It is a common mistake to believe that an emergency implies instant action rather than timely action.

Employees do not Understand the Importance of the Process

Yet another common problem in the IT world: Since most of the time, people deal with technology and use technology processes, they do not give due importance to service-management processes. Due to this attitude and misconception, they try to circumvent the process.

Advice – establish process compliance audits to detect quality and compliance issues, and to identify serial offenders. Make track leads accountable for enforcing process compliance within their team.

Role-Mapping is Ambiguous

Every actor in the process must know what task he is expected to perform and in what manner. A person may undertake multiple roles. This is usually done during process implementation— you map the roles to individuals and provide training for that role.

Advice – clearly define the roles and responsibilities, and explicitly designate the required roles to individuals.

Lack of Faith in the Process

Faith is believing in something without asking for an evidence. People demonstrate faith in many aspects of their daily business. When a passenger checks in at an airline counter and hands over the baggage, he has full faith that he will receive the baggage on the belt at the destination.

The passenger does not challenge the airlines systems and processes. Human beings take a leap of faith in almost everything in life. Every day when a person steps out and switches on the ignition of his car, he believes that it will start. He does not plan his day based on what if it did not start. This is a leap of faith. We do many things the way we do, because we have faith that by doing so, it will work.

Without faith, life would be miserable. Therefore, it is essential for people to have faith in the processes to perform the prescribed tasks faithfully.

Another merit of faith is that it helps you achieve more, simply because energy is not wasted in inventing solutions to unfound problems! Of course, it is the responsibility of the process manager to earn that level of faith.

Advice – leverage use cases and stories to instill a process mindset, and to emphasize the benefits of following processes.

Process Itself was Inadequately Designed for Practice

Over the last decade, the ITIL phenomenon produced many process consultants who wrote great processes, but those processes could not be implemented completely. The main reason was that these consultants were not connected to the grass root of IT operations and ignored real-life constraints of operations.

Such processes were theoretical and great on paper, but not practically viable. While it is necessary to create a theory first, it is also equally necessary to translate theory into practice. In fact, all the technology that has been invented was first envisioned as theory, and only then could it come to practice. In other words, a validated and relevant theory would make a good foundation of process.

Advice - this can be addressed through process stakeholders participating in process design. Workshop during the design phase is the best instrument to ensure that the process does not remain theoretical.

Challenge the Status Quo

Over a period of time, people acquire certain behavioral patterns while working with existing processes. These patterns eventually become involuntary and instinctive ways of working.

Many processes however demand radical changes in the way of working. These changes may be necessary for business but become difficult for actors in the processes. Blindly sticking to the status quo will inhibit your ability to do things better and obtain better results.

Below is a study that illustrates the same.

Two researchers conducted an experiment with a group of monkeys. Four monkeys were placed in a room with a tall pole at the center. Suspended from the top of the pole were a bunch of bananas and other exotic fruits. One of the hungry monkeys started climbing the pole to get the bananas. But just as he reached out to grab one, he was blasted with a torrent of cold water from hidden nozzles. He could not withstand the trouble and quickly retreated. He made several attempts, but every time he was tamed by the cold shower.

He finally gave up on his attempt to grab the great food and instead settled for the easily available rotten and otherwise compromised food strewn on the floor. Every monkey made a similar attempt, and in turn each monkey was blasted with a torrent of cold water. After making several attempts, all the monkeys concluded that easy but compromised food was the only way to satisfy hunger and survive.

The researchers then removed the shower jets and also removed one of the monkeys from the room and replaced him with a new monkey. As the newcomer began to climb the pole, the other three monkeys grabbed him and pulled him down the pole to the ground. After trying to climb the pole several times and being pulled down each time by the other "seasoned" or experienced monkeys, the new monkey finally gave up and joined the bandwagon to survive on compromised food.

The researchers replaced the original monkeys one by one, and each time a new monkey was brought in, he would attempt to fetch the exotic fruits and would be dragged down by the seasoned monkeys before he could reach the fruits.

Eventually the room was filled with monkeys who had never received the cold shower. Yet none of them would climb the pole. And not even one of them knew the reason why!

Blind inheritance and adoption of old processes is often the reason of sticking to old ways of working without knowing the reason why: We receive a legacy of habits that we are actively discouraged from questioning.

Organization change-management is one of the key areas during the implementation that can address the issue of habit versus innovation. This is also tied to management's commitment – institutionalization of good process habits is a critical success factor to deal with this aspect of potential failure.

Functional Structure of the Organization is Inadequate.

Since it is the function that executes the process, an adequate functional structure must be in place to run the processes. An informal functional structure may exist, but if not formalized, it is likely to make the process informal and prone to failure.

For example, the service desk as a function is one of the essential requirements for a successful incident-management process. In most organizations, it does exist but it is not empowered. Even in case of good service desks, without any influence over the support groups, incident ownership breaks down.

Many times, process implementation demands organizational change also. It could be organizational transformation or change in the ways of working, sometimes radical changes. If those changes are not implemented along with the process, the process will not be successful.

For instance, during the implementation of a new security-management process that imposes some controls on technical-management groups and requires a formal hierarchical structure, it must be ensured that the technical groups are also reconciled to the new organization structure, roles and work equations.

4.1.5 Generally Observed Process Deficiencies

Incident Management

There are usually two sources of incidents; those reported by end-users and those detected by event-monitoring tools. The first step of incident management process is entirely different based on the incident source. When a user reports an incident, the customer, an external person assumes the role of "requestor." At the time of closure, explicit consent is obtained from the requestor to close the ticket. With this consent, we want to ensure that the delivered resolution really worked for the requestor.

If the incident is reported by event monitoring, then who will take up the role of requestor? Absolute clarity is required not only to register an incident but also to close the incident.

At the time of registering the incident, a variety of policies have a direct influence on the process. One of them is related to prioritization of incidents.

As per prevailing best practices, prioritization is decided by the combination of impact and urgency. With this approach, a customer should merely report the symptom, and based on the guidelines, the help desk should make a judicious decision about the priority of the incident

In most organizations however, prioritization is based on nothing but the severity of an incident, and there is often a dispute about the degree of severity. The customer insists that a higher value or degree of severity should be assigned to obtain a higher level of service. A mature process will provide clear guideline and protocols to handle such disputes.

Also open to interpretation are vague incident prioritization guidelines, which is a considerable process gap. For example, "Huge business impact: Disruption/breakdown of the work of multiple people or a business-critical application failure" will not be sufficient unless accompanied by specific examples such as 'Mail/Exchange/Citrix application malfunction at server level', 'Catastrophic spread of virus', or 'Order booking application halted'.

Even if this level of clarity is given, the supporting data may not be available. For example, the guideline refers to 'Tier 1 business-critical application' but the data or the list of applications may not be available.

There may also be disputes about the scope of service during the acceptance and registration of the incident. It is important to cover the policy in such cases.

Occasionally, there may be cases where the impact of an incident assessed at the time of registration may not be correct, and after initial diagnosis you may find that the impact was different from what it was originally assessed to be.

What should be the policy for upgrading or downgrading the impact value during an incident-management life cycle? This is very important because measurements and contractual obligations are based on priority.

Yet another policy is around the usage of pending status. In most systems, the duration of a pending state is not accounted for in SLA measurement. In such systems, there is a possibility of abusing the pending status.

In almost all organizations, there is something like 'Critical Incident Management' with a variety of processes built around it. Most of the time organizations define the role of critical incident manager but fail to empower her.

This role demands influence and authority across technology groups to mobilize resources on demand, and manage resolution efforts, but this is role is often designated to a junior person, making the process much less effective.

Incident management demands strong policies on some core matters of process, but most often these are ignored.

1. How will you measure the SLA for variable priority?
2. How will you handle prioritization disputes?
3. How do you handle scope related disputes?
4. How will you prevent the abuse of 'pending' status that pauses SLA?

Problem Management

Problem management is a highly misunderstood process. Most problem management processes are only special incident management processes. A commonly observed mistake in this regard is the differentiation between an incident and a problem.

Many times, the work-around itself is treated as the root cause of an incident, and problem management rarely focuses on the true root cause.

Another common issue is misunderstanding the role of the problem manager and investigator. In most cases, the problem manager role is not assigned to the right individual, and is reduced to a clerical role.

One of the most important obligations that needs to be served by problem management is the creation and maintenance of a Known Error Database (KEDB). However, this obligation is rarely being served. Technically, for every problem there must be a KEDB record if the root cause has been identified. Further, this KEDB record should be active till the permanent solution has been implemented.

A problem needs to be qualified before we invest time and effort in investigation, because not all the problems need to be investigated, but such qualification guidelines are missing in most implementations.

Even for the problems that have been investigated, we may not have immediate solutions. (Root cause analysis (RCA) identified, but solution not implemented.

Therefore, we should learn to live with problems; however, there must be an active work-around for every problem we are living with.

Most problem management processes talk only about solving the problem. However, a good implementation will also let you learn to live with a problem! It may sound odd, but the truth is that it is not viable to solve every problem, and learning to live with a problem is an important aspect of problem management.

In the application world, the word 'defect' is heard very often, and in fact defect is another name or terminology for problem. Ideally, all software should be defect-free; however, that level of perfection is rarely achieved.

Such perfection is not merely an IT matter; in many business situations, customers accept deficiencies (and 'non-showstopper" defects) and demand an early release. For example, the automation of single sign-on does not work, and the user must provide a password every time he accesses a secured content across multiple systems.

Besides this, technology remains the focus of problem management. But in majority of cases, the problem is not really with product or technology. It is with the process. If an application failed because data was not available, the root cause will often say 'batch job failure' but this is not the root cause. The root cause is somewhere in the event-management process or in the job configuration itself.

In most organizations, the law of conservation of problems prevails. "Problems cannot be eliminated or solved. They can only be transferred from one head to other". This law will prevail till the problem is pursued via a well-defined process and methodology to address the root cause.

Request Fulfillment

A successful request-catalog solution will depend on user profile data.

One of the common mistakes people make is that they focus on the service-request (SR) catalog but do not invest in the process of creating and maintaining user profiles.

There are compelling reasons to ensure that user profiles are accurately maintained using a tool for effective service management. This is a prerequisite for implementing an SR catalog system. In the SR environment, a good solution should accommodate several types of requests, which will lead to a variety of approval requirements such as the manager, the reviewer and the budget approver.

To automate these kinds of approvals, we need strong user-profile management in the process to determine the appropriate data source in a particular customer environment and design a solution.

A good solution also requires a strong data strategy, which makes the ITSM system use one unique ID for all purposes to avoid data-management overheads.

The following general points emphasize the need for a strong user-profile management solution:

1. Dependency of process on user profile: A process may break if a user profile has missing data. For example, a user submits an SR that requires cost-center approval, and the cost-center is not available in the user profile.

2. Maintaining the integrity of process: A process may deliver the wrong result if executed in a faulty manner. For example, the cost center is available, but was not correct; therefore, the wrong approval was obtained or wrong approval was attempted.

3. Good service experience to user: User profiles provide personal preferences or attributes that can be used to give a better experience.

For example, a VIP tag in a user profile enables the service provider to accord more importance to that customer.

4. Smooth operation of process: A user's building and cubicle location will enable onsite service to be provided more effectively.

5. Quality of customer service: Communication throughout the service transaction will use the contact data from the user profile.

6. Help in workload management: Based on physical location information derived from the profile, you can optimize multiple customer visits and improve logistics of service delivery.

7. Compliance help: You can track the privileges assigned to a user and support regulatory compliance.

A second, but no less important aspect, is to implement the process for managing the service catalog itself. No catalog will be static, and it will change with business needs. Some organizations do not understand catalog maintenance, and they do it like content management. Catalog management is quite different from content management.

Change Management

What is considered as 'change' is not often very well-defined. The scope of the process should be clear in terms of CI types, environments and a clear description of what is considered a change and what is not considered as a change.

A scope exclusion statement such as "Routine housekeeping activities that do not alter operating systems, utilities, or applications, but are designed to maintain the overall health and performance of the computing environment" would be sufficient in the process document but must be clearly illustrated in implementation with environment specific examples. There can be more specific examples such as defragmentation of disk drives, purging logs, or rebuilding database indexes.

The actual trigger for change management is not clearly answered in most implementations. Many organizations enable change controls only to maintain the integrity of the production environment. This implies that whatever happens before the change is not monitored. While this may work for the infrastructure layer, it is not suitable for application changes, and leads to the implementation of two change-management processes - one for infrastructure and one for application.

Application changes traverse through multiple environments and are tracked throughout their life cycles. Infrastructure changes do not have 'development' work, but they still need to be tested. A single process with different points of entry in the process cycle is preferred.

Another inconsistency in change management is with respect to the treatment of emergency changes. A common practice is to trigger an emergency change required to resolve a critical incident, but there is no enforcement. Also, unqualified and untested changes make their way through this weakness. The policy itself is not weak, but the implementation of controls is often weak.

Risk assessment of changes is very often inadequate. Most of the time 'technical' rather than stakeholders people perform the risk assessment which itself is a risk.

Besides this, the risks are often captured without supporting document and methodology. Risks are based on what a person thinks rather than what he knows, the data is usually not available or analyzed sufficiently when available.

This can usually be addressed by incorporating risk criteria and guidelines to drive consistency across groups and individuals.

Despite all the precautions and measures, changes may still fail in production. While the process needs to be designed to reduce the probability of failed changes, it also needs to provision for the policies about failed changes. The criteria of success or partial success (and thus partial failure) are not adequately established in many change-management processes. Also, the policies around failed changes (partially failed and completely failed) are often ambiguous.

Change management is also confused with release management. The fundamental concept that every release is a change, but every change is not a release, is not understood very well.

Asset, Configuration Item and Managed Object

A configuration item (CI) is a component of the infrastructure that produces or contributes to the production of an IT service. A CI is a component of IT infrastructure that needs to be managed because it has an impact on IT service. CMDB is a complex database, but configuration management is a relatively simple process.

An asset is an item that has economic value. An asset database is relatively simple, but the asset management process is complex, as it has a much longer lifecycle.

A managed object (MO) represents the operational properties of a CI related to operational behavior. It is the management view of the system resource subject to operational control. The event management process is the cornerstone of this operational control.

In operations, managed objects are dynamic in nature. For example, if the exchange server is up but the RPC service is hung, the e-mail service will be unavailable. Here, the Exchange Server as a CI has little relevance on event monitoring, but the RPC service as the managed object is far more relevant.

CMDB is a database and does not have value without a configuration management process. In almost all the cases, a tool is implemented, but not a process. CMDB and configuration management are not the same. CMDB is a database, and configuration management is the control process built around CMDB to maintain the accuracy, currency, and integrity of the data in the CMDB.

Similarly, discovery and data population is not CMDB creation. A discovery tool does not discover all the data that may be required to create a CMDB, and lot of 'data preparation' is required before the discovered data is ready to be used. Discovery is a very small part of a real CMDB project.

The integration of a discovery tool and CMDB is not configuration management; one also needs to take care of the other data that is not discovered.

A meaningful CMDB proposition should have at least three elements:

1. CMDB Design – the design of a data model and CMDB architecture will be driven by the purpose of the CMDB.
2. CMDB Baseline Creation - identifies multiple data sources, discovery, data preparation, and data loading.
3. Process Design - design and implementation of control processes.

In any CMDB implementation, the consulting and implementation cost will be many times the cost of tools.

Confusing Asset Management and Configuration Management

There is a lot of misconception around asset management and it gets confused with configuration management, primarily because of the tools mixing them up.

The irony is that ITIL V3 even contributed to this misconception with its

4 SERVICE OPERATIONS

'Service Asset and Configuration Management' process in ITIL V3. An asset management database (AMDB) and a CMDB are not the same.

Asset is a hardware product or software license that needs to be managed, because it has some economic value, and the AMDB is the database that provides information about IT assets. An AMDB will have information about economic attributes such as cost, depreciation, contract, and purchase date, but no information about relationships with other assets.

Configuration item is a component of IT infrastructure that need to be managed because it has an impact on IT services. CMDB will have information about technical attributes and configurations such as host name, IP address, and relationship with other CI, but no information about economic value.

An asset may or may not be a CI; conversely, a CI may or may not be an asset. AMDBs and CMDBs may share some common items such as data center devices, but different attributes. Some items such as end-user devices, and software licenses should only be included in an AMDB but not in a CMDB.

Some items such as clusters and logical systems may be included only in a CMDB but not in an AMDB (in cloud computing, a virtual machine is also a candidate for the AMDB).

The asset life cycle is significantly longer. A server can exist in the AMDB with a status of 'In Stock' but it will not exist in the CMDB till the asset status transits to 'Deployed'. Similarly, a decommissioned asset will not exist in a CMDB but exists in an AMDB.

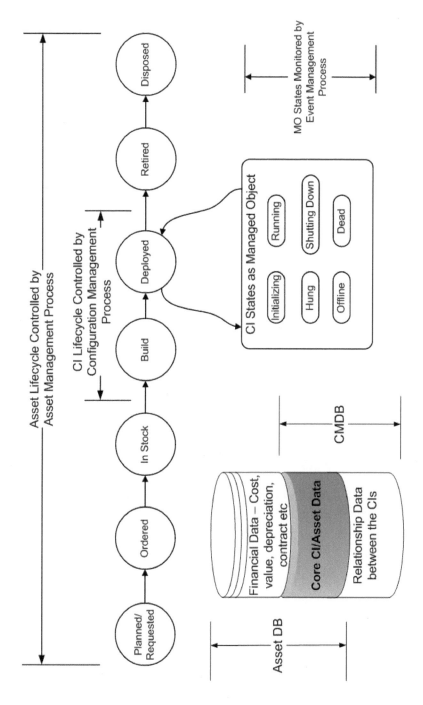

Figure 16: Asset, CI and managed Object

Asset discovery in itself does not constitute the asset-management process. Typical asset-management proposals (excluding software) will have two basic elements:

1. Asset database creation
2. Development and implementation of asset-management process

While the first part is much simpler, the second part is much more complex than the configuration-management process. The cost of implementing the asset management process is significantly higher than tool cost.

If the scope includes software, consider that asset-management software is comprehensive and very complex and typically includes the following:

1. Selection, standardization, and approval for software products (especially architectural and compatibility consideration).
2. Purchasing or otherwise obtaining software, such as downloading it for use.
3. Managing software installations, licenses, and contracts, including proof of ownership (very complex because of variety of licensing schemes)
4. Reclaiming licensed software for reuse (harvesting process).
5. Creating and maintaining a definitive software library (DSL).
6. Legal compliance and preventing unauthorized use.

Most asset-management software addresses only a part of the above processes.

Many IT organizations do not have a specific process for availability management, and hope that higher levels of availability will occur with the introduction of new and improved hardware. While fault-resistant hardware and data sharing can help availability, the root cause of poor availability can typically be found in two areas: IT processes and application design.

Availability management is a specific set of interrelated IT processes and tools that need to be viewed and managed from a single vantage point to maintain the highest possible level of service delivery. IT processes such as change management and backup and recovery management have a direct impact on availability, while other processes such as managing configuration changes may only have an indirect impact.

Following is a list of processes and how they support availability. Event management process is the most important and placed at the top of the list.

Activities Supporting Availability	Governing Process
Proactively monitor availability in real time and take actions on alarms	Event management
If availability incident occurs, resolve as quickly as possible	Incident management
Proactively identify problems and Eliminate	Problem management
Control configuration changes and maintain the system up to date	Change management
Regular backups	Operational activities
Perform design audits while releasing new services	Release management
Establish availability requirements and availability SLAs	SLM process
Ensure that increased consumption does not impact availability	Capacity management
Component failure impact analysis (and design audits) and risk mitigation	Availability management

The only activities directly in scope of availability management are availability risk assessment and management, and implementing cost-justifiable countermeasures. Both are rarely performed.

Event-Management Process

Event management as a formal process is rarely recognized and implemented in most IT organizations. What exists in the name of event management is the monitoring tool implementation.

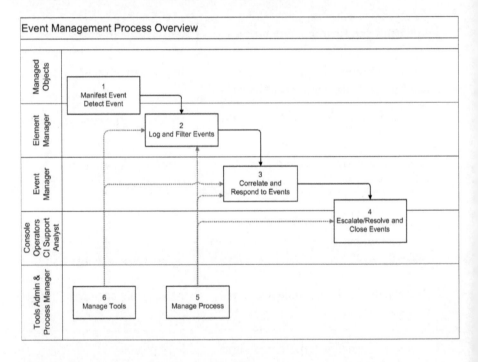

Figure 17: Event management Process and Role Overview

The key takeaway from the above diagram is that roles not only belong to the person, but also to the machine. If the machine or the CI itself is not designed properly, event monitoring will not work. If a CI does not have instrumentation for a defined managed object, it cannot be monitored, as the first step itself will fail.

The following deficiencies are commonly observed with event management implementation:

1. The part of the event management process that can be done by the tool configuration is implemented, but the remaining are ignored. This means that event monitoring is implemented, but not the process for full event lifecycle management.

2. Sub process 5 as depicted in Figure 17 is ignored almost everywhere. The process is not managed. There might be some ad-hoc reconfigurations, but once the 'tool' is implemented, everything is deemed as completed.

3. Sub process 6 is ad-hoc and not well governed. Therefore, the process loses its efficiency and effectiveness, and that is reflected in IT operations in terms of inconsistent workloads.

4. Most implementations are based on generic monitoring thresholds, and these are not customized to the CI type, CI function and customer requirement. The correct threshold value should be derived from the health model of the object. For example, if a server is being used as a file server, then 25% CPU utilization could be an alarm; however, if the server is being used for transaction processing, then even 75% CPU utilization could be normal. If both are being monitored against the same parameter, it could result in missed alerts and false alarms.

5. Another common issue is the inability to differentiate among events, alarms, and incidents. Creation of an automated incident for

unqualified events is very common. People do so because it can be done and because vendors say so.

6. And finally, there is no concept of a process and system health model for maintenance. 'Manage tool and manage process' activity in Figure 17 is mostly ignored.

Service-Level Management (SLM) Process

The implementation of SLM processes is usually limited to the measurement and reporting of SLAs. However, we do not focus on the benchmarking of service-level requirements against SLAs as well as the benchmarking of delivery capabilities against SLR.

While SLAs are defined, the measurement logic is left wide open for interpretation. OLAs are frequently ignored and that leaves a big crack in SLAs.

Some SLAs demand application availability more than system availability on which the application is running!

Knowledge Management (KM)

A common mistake is the failure to differentiate between knowledge and data. Most of the times, data is treated as knowledge, and that directly impacts the usability and the purpose of knowledge management.

Invariably, knowledge management is deemed as the deployment of collaborative applications. Deployment of technology such as groupware application, collaborative applications, data mining, and data warehousing applications is not knowledge management. Technology does not create knowledge. It only facilitates knowledge management.

In fact, the concept of knowledge management was born because the technology to manage it became affordable. KM is the process of managing the entire lifecycle of knowledge, from developing or discovering the knowledge from raw data, storing it, and distributing it to within the organization to help attain business goals.

Customer Satisfaction (CSAT)

This aspect is largely misunderstood and lacks focus in most IT operations. While customer-satisfaction measurement is one of the best tools available for real service improvement, it is also the most underutilized tool.

We all know that customer satisfaction is one of the key metrics in IT service outsourcing contracts, and there must be a mechanism to find out whether our customers are really satisfied or not. Variety of measurements are established, but they lack fundamentals.

Most measurements are based on the responses to a few questions in the survey embedded in the incident-management process. In fact, it is a very good idea to do so, but that is where the value of this idea ends. The closure moments of a service-support transaction offer an opportunity to solicit feedback, and one must use this opportunity in such a way that it goes beyond the narrow purpose of measuring the service desk or the success of that transaction alone.

What happens most often is that the performance of the service desk is judged based on the customer-satisfaction (CSAT) measurements. Customer response on surveys should be deemed as the response to overall service delivery and service support rather than viewing it just as the feedback for the service desk. In fact, the customer may be dissatisfied because of multiple reasons. Here are a few scenarios:

A customer reported an incident that was resolved in time, and the solution did work as expected. In the entire process, his call was answered promptly; the incident was promptly diagnosed as a virus attack on his

4 SERVICE OPERATIONS

laptop. The technician took prompt action and cleaned the virus; resolution was delivered in a timely manner, and the solution worked perfectly. Yet, the customer responded through survey that he was dissatisfied.

The reason for his dissatisfaction was that the virus entered the system even though there were all kind of protections installed and maintained by corporate IT! This was a clear failure of the security-management process.

In another situation, several users were dissatisfied when an e-mail server was down. All these customers made desperate calls to the service desk, which promptly responded and assigned the ticket to the mail server team and regularly updated the user community about the progress. Finally, when the e-mail was restored within the SLA target, a satisfaction survey was sent to each user who had reported the issue. While some of them appreciated that they were kept informed about the progress, several were dissatisfied and commented that the e-mail was not reliable. Here, a failure of availability management caused customer dissatisfaction.

Customer satisfaction is more a matter of meeting or exceeding customer expectations rather than the actual, contracted service levels. It is possible that the SLA is exceeded but you still fail on customer satisfaction because the customer's expectation was higher than the SLA. Conversely, we could receive customer appreciation for the service that has breached the SLA just by managing the expectation appropriately. If nothing is done to set the expectation, then it will be set by default, and that may impact customer satisfaction. Expectations should be managed by the SLM process and dynamically supported by the other ITSM process.

To avoid customer dissatisfaction due to wrong expectation, it is important to proactively set the right expectation. One of the easy methods to do so is to communicate the expected resolution time based on the contracted service levels at the time of communicating the ticket number. This can be automated in the system. Response should be analyzed in the context of the entire set of data, the transaction data that invoked the survey as well as the indirectly related data.

Furthermore, for an IT service-improvement agenda, feedback and action items come from customer dissatisfaction. Therefore, the measurement of customer dissatisfaction becomes more important than customer satisfaction itself.

The best time to conduct a customer satisfaction survey is when the experience of a service is fresh in the minds of customers. If we wait to conduct a survey, the customer's response may be less accurate. They may have forgotten some of the details. So, the approach should be to collect the response within a week of completing the service transaction, the survey should be done before the memory of the experience fades away.

Some of the common mistakes or deficiencies in this area are as follows:

1. **The kind of questions people ask:** "Was the technician knowledgeable?" is the most common question. Are you measuring the knowledge of technician, or you are measuring customer satisfaction? How you can rely on the judgment of an end user on the technical skill of the technician? How do you know that he or she is qualified to measure the knowledge of the technician? What is the purpose of asking such a question? Is the customer interested in the knowledge of technician or good service? A highly knowledgeable person does not guarantee a good service. The total contribution of knowledge toward customer satisfaction is such a small part that to assess that would waste an opportunity to obtain feedback.

2. **The interpretation derived from the response.** The conclusion you draw from the response is an even larger problem. So, if an end user stated that the technician was not knowledgeable, then you would conclude that the person requires training. Why would you not

conclude that the right person is in the wrong job? Or why would you not conclude that the manager who hired him did the mistake, and that the manager was less qualified than the user to assess the knowledge of the technician? Even if the conclusion on training was correct, and you train the person, you still cannot guarantee that it will lead to customer satisfaction.

The problem with some common methods of surveying customer satisfaction is that unreliable data is collected, and then incorrect conclusions are made.

So, what is the right thing to do?

Satisfaction is highly subjective and personal. Therefore, do not attempt to measure individual factors (such as a technician's skill) through the customer. Instead, measure the satisfaction level as determined by the customer himself, the end result. Only two questions will suffice:

1. How satisfied are you with the service?
2. Is there anything that we can do to improve the service?

Further, collect the databased on the reasons for customer's dissatisfaction, and then analyze it correctly. Service desks are often judged by customer-satisfaction measurements. The fact is customer experience is the interpretation of the service as a whole and must be interpreted in that context:

If CSAT is bad because of repeated failures, then it is the failure of problem management, not the service desk.

> If CSAT is bad because of performance (application or network), then it is the failure of capacity management process.

> If CSAT is bad because the customer was expecting faster-than-SLA

service, then it is the failure of SLM process, not the service desk.

If CSAT is bad because the quality of the solution is bad, then it is the failure of problem management process, not the service desk.

If CSAT is bad because of a timeliness issue, then it is the failure of incident management process, not the service desk.

If CSAT is bad because the service was not reliable, then it is the failure of availability management process, not the service desk.

4.2 Function

4.2.1 Service Desk: Most Visible Function

A service desk is the prime customer-facing function in an IT organization. The need for a 'strategic' service desk has been promoted in several forums and well recognized across the industry at all levels.

However, when it comes to practice, this is rarely adopted. All the service desks are at operational level, not even at a tactical level. In various discussions, though, IT management in all the organizations wants to claim that they have a 'strategic service desk'.

The service desk is entrusted with the responsibilities of managing the incident life cycle but they do not have influence over resolution groups.

An ideal service desk has the capability to help users obtain the full value of technology, but unfortunately, this is the place where there maximum cost-cutting occurs, and the service desk is deemed to be the lowest rank in an IT organization. This is the case almost everywhere!

Here is an example of an empowered service desk. In this organization, every month, the CIO came to the service desk and spent an hour in the role of a service desk agent, took calls and logged tickets. This gave him the opportunity to understand what exactly is being delivered to customers, and whether all the services produced and delivered by application and infrastructure are usable or not, and to what extent they are usable.

The service desk is the stage that provides an opportunity to listen to the customer. Through this, the CIO was gaining valuable insight to develop IT strategy to serve the purpose of the end users.

4.2.2 Other Functions Embedded in Processes

While service desk and command centers are the two prominent functions, there are embedded roles in each process that are performing process activities.

Processes do require a role to perform a process, a task or an activity. If roles are not assigned in the process, you can say that the process is not implemented. Incident resolver, problem investigator, critical incident manager, change implementer etc. are the typical roles.

Is your Team Functionally Complete?

You have track leads for managing the technology but is technical line management sufficient for managing services? Some of the roles like capacity analyst, availability manager, catalog manager etc. are usually not established and results in a gap.

You do not need a full-time person for every role. For example, a typical server administrator is also an incident resolver for server incidents, change implementer for changes on server, and problem investigator for root cause analysis for incidents on servers.

These are three different processes and three different roles, but mapped to the same person. Have you ensured that roles like availability manager, capacity analyst, catalog manager etc. are mapped to a designated individual in your team and that the person is trained adequately to perform those roles?

In other words, you can rely upon your technology track leads to ensure the reliability of the technology but you need to take the primary role of a cross functional service manager across all the tower-based teams that you lead and manage.

4.3 Tools

Tool is the third pillar of service management.

However, a fool with a tool is still a fool. In other words, implementation of a bad process through a tool, only helps in performing a bad job faster and with lesser effort.

Note: The intent of this section is not to explain the need for tools, or how tool administration and maintenance is performed.

5 KEY HYGIENES OF OPERATIONAL HEALTH

Right from our childhood, we are taught about hygiene as the fundamental conditions or practices conducive to maintaining body health and preventing disease. Top five hygiene that we have learned are cleanliness, sanitation, sterility, purity and disinfection. Likewise, for IT operational health we are listing top six hygiene namely Event Monitoring and Control, Patch Management, Batch Management, Incident Management & Critical Incident Management ,Backup & Restore and DR Management. This list is backed by our experience of running operations of many customers for many years. Of course, more factors can be added to list, but we have chosen to elaborate the top six factors that we believe are the most important contributor to operational health.

5.1 Event Monitoring and Control

IT systems, components, and services usually do not deteriorate abruptly, but they deteriorate gradually. The rate of decay is dependent upon a range of factors, such as what something is made of, how it is used, and the environment in which it is operated.

Regardless, degradation below the usable level can be detected ahead of time. Event detection and monitoring is thus the crucial early warning system for IT operations and service management. The root cause of incidents and problems lie in events that may or may not have been detected. The maturity of the event management process will bring in visible change in operations and shift the paradigm of operation from crisis management to planned sustenance.

Event Management Process and Roles

While much of the processing is done in the earlier stages, the event lifecycle status tracking is applied only after an event record is generated. This event record could denote an alert or an incident. Event status tracking is primarily required to track the actions on qualified events. These actions are necessary to eliminate the real and potential threats on service availability.

This is illustrated through Figure 18

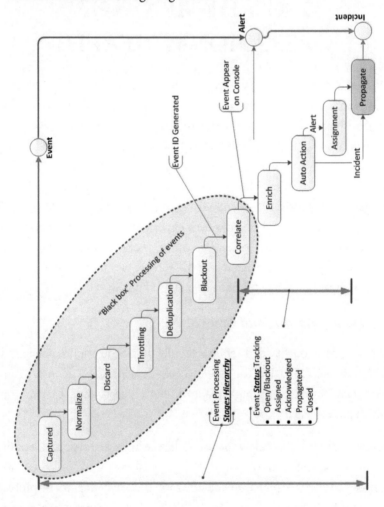

Figure 18: Event processing

Creating Incident Tickets from Event

If you are only focused on managing the technology, then receiving an alert and fixing the problem is enough. However, technology management is not sufficient – you need to manage services. That requires understanding the impact of an incident on services and taking appropriate steps that could go beyond repair actions. Let us illustrate this with a hypothetical scenario.

Event monitoring detects an incident on an enterprise e-mail server indicating a server outage. A notification is immediately triggered to the server management group. Someone sees the notification and takes the responsibility to fix it. The SLA is two hours for this critical outage, and the server is fixed within the SLA. Is everyone happy? Not necessarily. These actions focus on the technology, not the service.

With service management focus, you would immediately notify the service desk in addition to fixing the server (usually through automated integration between the event management and incident management processes). As soon as the service desk sees the critical incident in red, they will get ready for the flood of end-user calls because of the e-mail outage. These service-oriented actions include bulletin board announcements on the portal, programming the ACD for outage announcement for incoming calls, keeping users and customers updated, management escalations, etc. When a user calls in to report the issue, he will be told by the service desk that "Yes, we are aware of this issue, and so and so is working on it, and the estimated time is xyz."

All these activities need a strong and consistent service management process. Integration between event management and incident management is the most desirable solution, and it is very common.

Although this solution is perceived as and referred to as tool integration, it is in the process integration where event management process and incident management process share data on specific conditions.

Event Management in Cloud World

Monitoring and control in cloud is as much applicable as to any IT infrastructure. The big difference is who the service provider is and what service they are delivering. An IaaS service provider delivering infrastructure service will monitor and control events for their infrastructure and an IaaS customer will only monitor and control the services above that layer.

Similarly, a PaaS provider will monitor and control events on the runtime environment, in addition to the infra layer and the user will only monitor the application layer.

If you are consuming through virtual machines on the cloud and opted for 'unmanaged' service from the cloud service provider, then it is your responsibility to manage events at the OS layer, as well as the patch level.

5.2 Patch Management

Before the widespread adoption of Microsoft server operating systems at the enterprise level, patch management was an 'install and forget' practice; once deployed, many systems were seldom or never updated.

The rise of worms and malicious code-targeting known vulnerabilities on unpatched systems, especially Microsoft operating systems, and the resultant downtime and expense they bring has forced organizations to focus on patch management.

Along with these threats, increased emphasis on governance and regulatory compliance (such as HIPAA, Sarbanes-Oxley) has also forced enterprises to gain better insight and control over their systems. Also, pervasive interconnections with the outside world has also made it critical to secure your system with the latest patches.

While the issue of patch management has technology at its core, it is clear that focusing only on technology to solve the problem is not the answer. Installing patch-management software or vulnerability-assessment tools without supporting guidelines, and requirements will be a wasted effort that will further complicate the situation.

Instead, solid patch-management programs will leverage technological solutions with policy and operations based components that work together to address each organization's unique needs. And, this is what is being addressed through the patch-management process.

5 KEY HYGIENES OF OPERATIONAL HEALTH

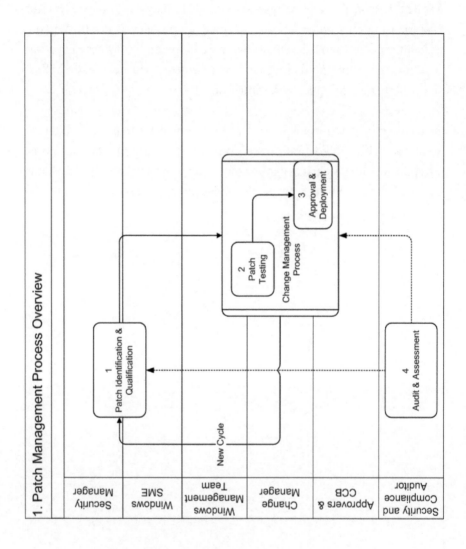

Figure 19: Patch management process and role overview

5.3 Batch Management

Batch Job Scheduling has been one of the major works of IT infrastructure since the early mainframe systems. It is the task of controlling an unattended background program execution of jobs. This is commonly called batch scheduling or batch processing, and in today's world it is referred to as workload automation.

Workload automation has two primary parts:

1. Build and Schedule Jobs
2. Run Jobs

Both parts are explained in detail with the help of Figure 20 on the next page.

5 KEY HYGIENES OF OPERATIONAL HEALTH

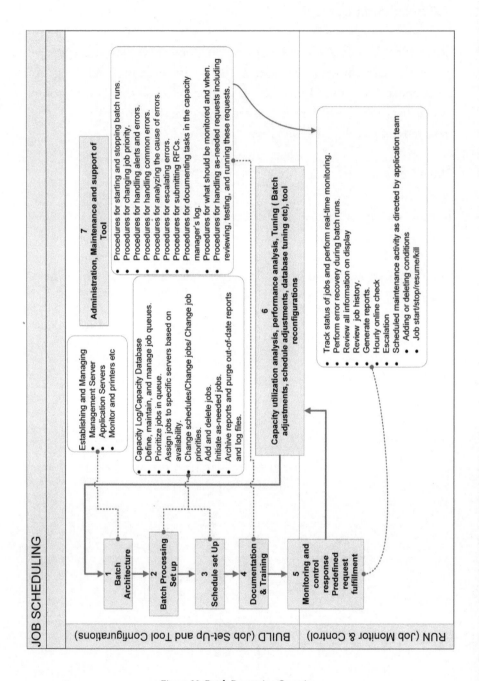

Figure 20: Batch Processing Overview

Job Monitoring and Control in Infra Outsourcing

Typically, the build part is owned and implemented by the customer, and the run part along with tool administration and support is outsourced to a service provider. Deficiency or poor quality in building and deployment will often appear as issues in operations.

These issues are the symptoms of the root cause which can be traced back to improper deployment or badly maintained control procedures for application specific jobs.

Job error handling procedures are out of date and not maintained. As a result, the execution of those procedures do not resolve error conditions and the issues gets escalated. It is very important to not only maintain tools, but also the procedures.

5.4 Incident Management & Critical Incident Management

All incidents should be monitored and their lifecycle should be managed. As shown in the below diagram, there are three key roles in Incident Management – the ITSM tool that does all the routine automated work, the service desk that acts as the owner of the incident, and the resolution owner of a ticket.

5 KEY HYGIENES OF OPERATIONAL HEALTH

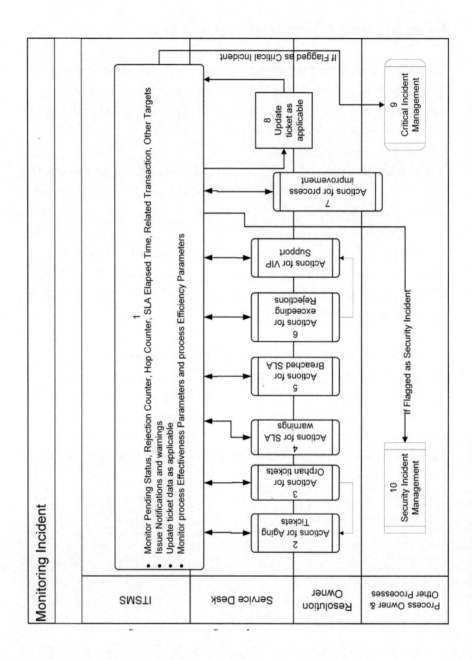

Figure 21: Incident Management Overview

It is expected that the incident management process will clearly define the policy and control response to incident management actions like action on pending ticket, action on aging ticket etc. If not, the SDM needs to define those policies before expecting consistent outcome from the incident management process.

When an Incident Becomes Critical

When an incident becomes a critical incident, a few additional roles pitch into action and that is – Critical Incident Manager (CIM), the service desk or command center, and the technical resolution owner.

A CIM is not a full-time designated person but a role that must be played by a senior person. It is recommended that none less than a track lead play this role. Since a critical incident can occur anytime, one has to cover the CIM role on 24x7 basis, and you will need at least 5 people in the team who are adequately trained for this role.

The key job responsibilities and qualification of a critical incident manager include:

- Has the influence and authority to get resources on demand from technical groups.
- Responsible for interfacing with service owner and technical teams to formulate a resolution action plan.
- The capability to drive issues toward resolution.
- Ability to manage stakeholders and publish periodic notifications on incident status and progress.
- Invoke parallel efforts for providing a workaround for service resumption where primary resolution efforts are time consuming.

Critical Incident Manager is a ROLE – NOT a Full Time Job

A critical incident can occur at any time and needs 24x7 support. At least

5 people are needed to ensure full coverage.

The typical lifecycle of a critical incident lasts for about 4 hours. In most cases, the SLA is 4 hours, but it is resolved on an average in 2 hours. Add the reporting and follow-up task, overhead like closure communication and initiation of problem investigation (not root cause analysis), this will make it approximately 4 hours.

In a typical organization, there could be five critical incidents in a week. So, the approximate time spent on the CIM role is 20 hours per week. If you distribute this workload across five people, it would make this a workload of 4 hours per week, per person. This is just 10% of the workload of a person. It is therefore a no brainer to conclude that employing a dedicated person only for critical incident management does not make much sense.

Best practice is to assign the role of CIM to senior track leads. In any engagement, one needs to identify five track leads or persons of equivalent caliber and assign them the role of CIM. When a critical incident occurs, one of those available persons wears the hat of the CIM. She will resume regular work after the critical incident is closed. If the track leads are not able to take this role or are not willing to take this role, then consider them unfit for their job. Occasionally, the service delivery manager may also be required to play the role of a critical incident manager.

If there are too many critical incidents that require multiple full-time persons, it is okay for Fortune 100 customer who have global operations with many critical applications in their portfolio. If that is not the case, review the critical incident criteria - they are most likely not right and unqualified incidents are likely being treated as critical incidents. It also indicates that there is a significant problem in operations and problems are not being solved.

Critical Incident Management in Multi-Supplier and Cloud World

Critical incident management across multi-supplier is primarily a SIAM responsibility as it requires higher level of influence and authority across multiple suppliers.

5.5 Backup and Restore

Backing up data requires copying and archiving computer data, so that it is accessible in case of data deletion or corruption. Data can only be recovered if it has been backed up. Data backup is a form of disaster recovery and should be part of any disaster recovery plan, although backup requirements for DR is more comprehensive.

Nowadays a lot of data can be backed up when using cloud storage, but legacy data backup and restore solutions are still running predominantly in enterprises.

Traditional vs Cloud Backup:

Today, safeguarding technology assets is not a choice but a necessity for businesses. Due to criticality and importance of data and systems, backup strategy has always formed the core of any enterprise IT function.

Over a period of time, traditional backup solutions and methodologies have undergone a substantial change. Traditionally, backup systems have been plagued with physical intervention, different and physically separated devices, proximity constraints etc.

These constraints are being mitigated by cloud based backup systems. Taking advantage of connectivity, cloud based backup systems have not only enabled the ease of performing backups, but also increased the agility, reliability and scalability of backup solutions as a whole.

Cloud based backup solutions are increasingly becoming popular due to low cost of ownership, absence of heavy upfront investment and minimal maintenance requirement.

Besides low cost of ownership, cloud based backup systems are increasingly benefitting from automation. Automation on cloud is making backup features and functions increasingly intuitive and simple.

Cloud Backup is becoming the de-facto standard for. Enterprises that have already adopted cloud based backup systems are witnessing its benefits over traditional backup systems.

5.6 DR Management

Disaster Recovery (DR) or IT Service Continuity Management (ITSCM) plans for handling unexpected major service outages, often referred to as disaster planning. IT service continuity affects business continuity (business impact analysis).

IT Service Continuity Management is closely related to the management of continuity on the business side, often referred to as business continuity management.

Continuity planning involves considering risk, threat and vulnerability. DR process analyzes different recovery options for recovering services. The result is an IT Service Continuity Plan. Prime responsibility for managing continuity in the event of a disaster or major outage lies with the Crisis Management Team

Cloud for Disaster Recovery

Cloud-based DR strategy and solutions have been gaining popularity and adoption in recent times. Organizations are waking up to this simple, efficient and low-cost option vis-à-vis non-cloud DR solutions characterized by high upfront cost, and significant resources.

There are multiple approaches for enabling cloud-based disaster recovery. Organizations may choose one of these approaches, contingent to their business needs and service requirements.

Any DR strategy requires a well-crafted approach to address an organization's DR requirements. The DR approach may include risk analysis, identification of priority assets, and choosing the right partners who can provide the requisite DR solution.

Cloud providers have been continuously improving their disaster recovery services, making them more flexible, configurable and automated. Most cloud-based DR comes with multiple options that enable different RPO (Recovery Point Objectives) and RTO (Recovery Time Objectives) based on the organization's requirements.

This flexibility enabled by Cloud-based DR is a boon for organizations and should increasingly be used to protect and safeguard their critical assets. This has not only impacted the ease of using these services, but has also increased the efficiency of these services.

Another important aspect that a cloud-based DR makes easy to implement is the testing of a failover scenario. This is a critical aspect of DR setup which tends to get overlooked by organizations, due to testing constraints which may typically be associated with a non-cloud-based DR solution.

As failures and disasters are imminent, continuous testing of DR scenarios prepares an organization for any eventuality and ensures the safety of critical data and systems.

As we move into the next phase of technology adoption, characterized by IoT, Cloud and AI-based solutions, cloud is poised to be increasingly used for disaster recovery in both regulated and unregulated environments.

6 SERVICE DELIVERY IN MULTISOURCE ENVIRONMENT

The IT service landscape is getting increasingly complex and multivendor IT service is virtually unavoidable. Outsourcing is also increasing rapidly, and there are multiple variations of outsourcing ranging from partial outsourcing to full outsourcing.

In the 1990s, Application Service Providers (ASPs) stepped into the space of outsourcing with very limited solutions. ASPs were successful for a time, but they eventually went out of the business (in their original forms) for various reasons.

Managed service providers replaced ASPs, offering an expanded, more scalable and yet more conservative approach towards IT outsourcing.

Now, a matured cloud model is in place with many service providers. Cloud is not only scalable, but commercially appealing as well. Therefore, the outsourcing model has acquired a high-degree of maturity and acceptance in the last few years. These days, IT outsourcing relationships are seen more as strategic partnerships than subcontracts.

Almost all the large companies use multiple vendors and system integrators – a practice called multi-sourcing to deliver on strategic initiatives and operational activities.

6 SERVICE DELIVERY IN MULTISOURCE ENVIRONMENT

In fact, multi-sourcing is one of Gartner's top trends in recent years. Gartner explores the challenges:

The multivendor model for IT services is complex and requires orchestration between vendors that are often fierce competitors. This orchestration requires the enterprise to establish a multi-sourcing delivery model that provides visibility and transparency into multiple vendor systems and processes. It becomes increasingly complex when both internal and external sources deliver services to the enterprise.

As a result, the role of a Multi-Sourcing Services Integrator (MSI) emerges. The client organization, a third party, or one of the vendors delivering services, can perform this role. The role however, is not very mature, requires investments in industry frameworks (such as IT Infrastructure Library), IT Service Management and Quality, and will increase the administrative costs of outsourcing and delivering services.
(Source: Gartner, Outsourcing Trends)

IT service management requires a completely new approach when it comes to outsourcing and multivendor relationships, as they will become the norm in the future.

IT infrastructure Library (ITIL) and Gartner view the challenges of service integration from a vendor management perspective. ITIL has provided valuable guidance on outsourcing models and vendor management.

However, we believe that vendor management is only a partial approach towards service integration. You need vendor management—it is an essential requirement—but you also need to manage services from the vendor. Vendor management and service management are not the same thing, but complementary, just like technology management and service management.

Considering that multi-sourcing is an established norm, organizations need to adapt to the new approach towards service management and service integration, as an integral part of multi-sourcing.

6.1 Need for Service Integration & Management (SIAM)

In the ITIL world, there is a service customer who is different from the consumer, and a service provider (the enterprise IT service provider by default is CIO of an organization). There is a Service Level Agreement (SLA) between these two parties, namely the service provider and the customer.

The service provider has internal groups and external contracts, so there is an Operational Level Agreement (OLA) between internal groups and an Underpinning Contract (UC) between the enterprise and external service providers including product vendors.

Unfortunately, the real world is not that simple. In the real world, there are multiple service providers who themselves can sub-contract. To manage service management equations in the real world, you need a real-world picture.

We have established a representative view with the following entities in the equation as shown in Figure 22.

6 SERVICE DELIVERY IN MULTISOURCE ENVIRONMENT

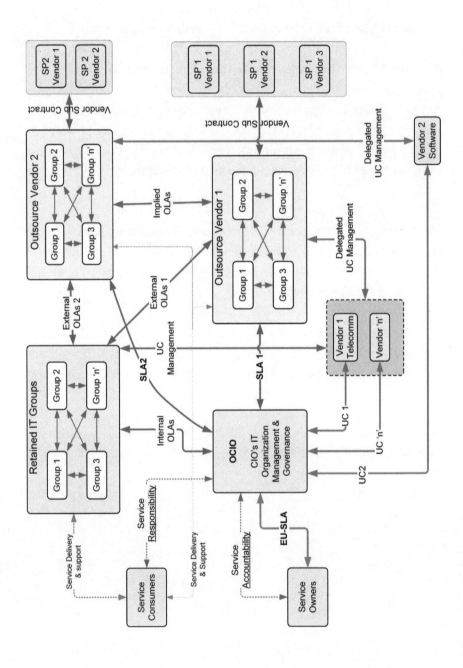

Figure 22: Complex Service Management Equation

1. Service Consumer: Usually the end user—an employee or the contractor in an organization. This is well defined in ITIL.
2. Business Service Owner: the business customer who defines the service, signs the SLA, and pays for the service. ITIL defines this role as a 'customer' of the service.
3. OCIO (Office of CIO): It is the CIO's IT organization that is responsible and accountable to the business and service consumers. OCIO is the 'deemed service provider' and this role is also responsible for service governance and multivendor governance.
4. Retained IT Groups: Internal functional groups, usually technology-based, managing specific technology areas and providing some of the services.
5. Service Providers (Outsourcing Vendors): These vendors provide some of the services to users on behalf of the deemed service provider—the CIO's IT organization. They interact with service consumers.
6. Vendors: Product vendors who deliver specific products—hardware or software—rather than services. This includes service providers who deliver a boxed outcome such as telecom service. They do not interact with service consumers.
7. Subcontractors: Outsourcing vendors may have some subcontractors. They work behind the scenes on behalf of the outsourcing vendor, and are not visible to any other party in the equation. We deliberately keep them outside our framework and only acknowledge their existence to relate with the real-world scenarios, but consider them hidden behind outsourcing vendor.

With these players in the service landscape, default ITIL definitions cannot be applied. We need to modify those definitions to apply them to the real world.

Typical View of Complex Service Management Equations

Following are the key elements in equation among these roles:

1. EU-SLA: The end-user SLA is the end-to-end agreement between the Office of Chief Information Officer (OCIO) and the end user. The service provider in this case is the OCIO. In ITIL terminology, it is an SLA. We are naming it EU-SLA to differentiate it from the SLA that OCIO signs with another company—the outsourcing vendor. EU-SLAs are defined and signed by the service owner—the representative of the business that is being served by the IT.

Most IT organizations have the role of a business partner who represents business to the IT. There are multiple business partners usually for each business function. Business partners not only sign the EU-SLA but also agree to provide the funds for producing and supporting the service as per the cost model. Though it is "internal" within the organization, it carries all the attributes of a contractual SLA.

2. SLA: this term is most commonly expressed and understood as the contractual SLA between the OCIO and the outsourcing service-provider organization. Many times, SLAs are defined to work as if they were EU-SLA, but that is not necessary. OCIO will have one contract with each outsourcing vendor and, consequently, at least one set of SLAs with each vendor.

We term these as SLA1, SLA2, and so on. The primary reason to introduce EU-SLA and SLA terminologies is to eliminate the possibilities of confusion in real-world understanding. The people in procurement, program management, vendor management, and legal departments (or even most of IT Operations) do not follow ITIL terminology, and for all practical purposes, this is an SLA for them.

3. OLA: ITIL teaches us that there ought to be an OLA to support the SLA. OLAs are not visible to service consumers but are designed to work in collaboration of internal teams to meet the SLAs. OLAs are supposed to be internal in the ITIL world. In our framework, the outsourced vendor is

providing the service on behalf of the CIO; therefore, they are logically an internal party for this purpose. However, in real terms, they are the external parties; therefore, we have differentiated OLAs as follows:
a. Internal OLA: the OLA as defined by ITIL and applicable to retained IT groups in the organization.
b. External OLA: the OLA defined between internally retained IT groups and the outsourcing vendor.
c. Implied OLA: the OLA between two outsourcing vendors who need to collaborate because of individually different SLAs with the customer. These two vendors do not have direct agreements, but it is 'implied' because of a common customer.

4. UC: The underpinning contract is the ITIL terminology used for the contract with external vendors to support the SLA. In our framework, we retain the original definition and meaning of UC but differentiate how internal or external groups will manage them.

In real life, there will be more than two outsourcing vendors and some of them could be cloud service vendors who can make the equations even more complex. Cloud service vendors have the characteristics of outsourcing vendors, product vendors, and managed service providers that multiplies their complexity. Key points to note are as follows:

1. OCIO as the service-provider organization is responsible for delivering the services to the service consumer and accountable to the service owners (business representative) on behalf of all the parties; that includes the internal groups, outsourcing vendors, and all the other vendors.

2. OCIO will usually own the strategy and design, including architecture, and select product vendors that meet the organization's architecture standards. These are UCs, but technology specific groups in organization will manage these vendors.

For example, server management group will manage the UC with the server vendor. Database group will manage the UC with database product vendor and so on. If a group that is managing the UC is external, then it is termed as the delegated UC management, because the CIO has delegated to manage the contract and obtain the services as specified in the contract.

3. If there is some deficiency in the UC, then it will impose corresponding deficiency in the SLA as well for which the outsourcing vendor is accountable. Therefore, the SLA not only requires OLA but also the UC to be compatible.

The Need for Service Integration

The number of individuals in service delivery and service support organizations could be in thousands. Even though they are organized in groups, the number of groups themselves could be in hundreds.

It is therefore impossible that every person contributing towards service delivery would have a holistic view of the services. Every individual performs the work with full knowledge of their individual part, but that is merely a fragmented view of the complete service.

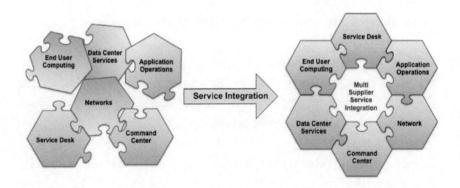

Figure 23: Need of SIAM

With an incomplete view, each vendor may be good in isolation, but collectively, things do not add up to make a complete service. Although every individual component of the service works, the end result falls through the cracks because of varied processes and ways of working adopted by different vendors.

Often, people in these situations know that there is a problem, but they do not know how to figure it out. The sum of individual parts is less than the whole. For all intents and purposes, one plus one in this scenario is less than two because the efforts of two service providers do not add up completely.

Thus, in addition to the individual services, you also need service integration that will bring harmony within each service component. Service integration will provide an organized structure for the collection of individual systems and component, and effectively defines a deterministic outcome. Service integration will provide a seamless service experience to the service consumers.

Service integration makes the outcome result-oriented, as opposed to the deliverable oriented output of individual groups, working with a fragmented view of the service.

In other words, service integration changes the equation and ensures that the whole is greater than the sum of its parts.

One example is cloud file share as a service. Cloud file sharing as a service provides a single front-end client and a consumption platform for end users. They might use multiple cloud storage providers like AWS or Azure Storage to store the files, but it is transparent to the end-user. The client abstracts the transport of data, but the payload might physically be stored in one of these cloud providers.

We see this in the airline industry also—if American Airlines has forty flights and US Airways has thirty flights, the combined carrier will have more than seventy flight choices because of connecting combinations.

An example of how customers are meeting the SIAM need informally is the Critical Incident Management (CIM) process. In most organizations, CIM process is defined and operated to bring about collaboration among multiple service providers.

When the moment of truth comes, someone rises to the occasion to assume the SIAM role and bind different technology SMEs together for the sole purpose of restoring the service as soon as possible. If your CIM process is well-defined, institutionalized and consistently achieving the goal, then you have implemented operational integration feature of SIAM for the CIM purpose.

Similarly, a formal SIAM solution will ensure operational integration for every process and much more than that.

6.1.2 SIAM Vs CFS

In a multi-tower technology setup, you must have a cross functional service group which will manage processes and tools that are common across the towers. Please note that process management and process operations are different. (An 'Incident Manager' is from an 'Incident Management Process Manager').

If the customer has a SIAM service organization, then CFS will interface with SIAM. If your organization is also a SIAM service provider, then the SIAM service delivery team must be outside the control of the service delivery manager who responsible for all the other towers. Merging the SIAM team into the same monolithic service delivery organization is a monumental mistake as shown in Figure 24.

6 SERVICE DELIVERY IN MULTISOURCE ENVIRONMENT

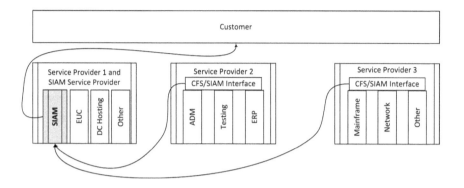

Figure 24: Wrongly organized teams in multi-supplier environment

The right design of SIAM is depicted in Figure 25. This design will ensure vendor neutral operation of SIAM service, and meet the intent of SIAM.

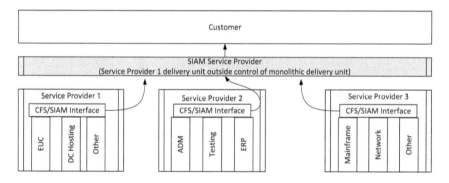

Figure 25: Correctly configured teams in multi-supplier environment

Typical Charter of SMO (Service Management Office)

SMO (Service Management Office) is the central function in SIAM.

This charter is applicable for directive SMO and can be scaled down for other types of SMO with corresponding reduction in the degree of integration. The principal charter of SMO is to orchestrate and facilitate collaboration among multiple service providers, thus ensuring coordination and delivery of integrated services.

This charter will invariably require unified processes and tools, and institutionalization of unified processes and tools would become an extended charter.

Unification of processes and tools is one of the cornerstones of service integration. Unification does not mean a single set of tools. It means an ability to trace a service transaction from start to finish. It can be the integration of multiple tools and processes of multiple service providers.

After unification of process and tools, SMO will orchestrate operations to meet the intent of unified service management processes, and would be responsible to keep them unified all the time through maintenance.

Three Parallel Functions - VMO, PMO and SMO

PMO - The Program/Project Management Office and VMO, the Vendor Management Office are the integral parts of OCIO. With the implementation of SIAM, the third parallel function – SMO will emerge.

It is important to explain the segregation of duties between these three parallel functions. VMO focuses on contracts, invoices, terms and conditions, vendor capabilities, and vendor qualifications etc.

The responsibilities of VMO includes:

1. Qualify the vendor- vendor worthiness, and good standing of vendor
2. Establish the MSA
3. Establish the framework of engagement
4. Establish the commercial contract
5. Establish the SOW
6. Validate invoice for delivery
7. Authorize payments

SMO focusses on 'what is delivered from the vendor'. The attributes managed by SMO are the warranty and utility of the service. The responsibilities of SMO include:

1. Qualify the services from the vendor- the service is fit for purpose and fit for use.
2. Define the outcome required from the vendor (help VMO to build SOW)
3. Verify deliverables from the vendor
4. Manage the operational activities of the vendor for service delivery and support.
5. Review the service performance with vendor.
6. Run service quality assurance panel with vendor.

PMO focuses on three attributes of the project – the budget, timeline, and deliverables (outcome). PMO may also deal with multiple vendors, but does so for the tenure of the project.

Let us illustrate with a typical example of datacenter migration project. This will involve participation from different vendors namely Server, application, network, storage, database etc. All these service providers will work under the direction of a program manager, collaborate with each other, and perform the task as directed by the program manager.

Once the project is closed, and goes into operation, all vendors are still required to collaborate and deliver the outcome daily under the direction of SMO. In other words, SMO is the ongoing PMO.

Additional Functional Prerequisites

In our integration model, we consider two additional functions as the prerequisite for implementing service integration. These are command center and the service desk.

Service Desk

Service Desk is a very well recognized function since ITIL promoted the best practice of a Single Point of Contact (SPOC) for all the users of IT Services. Service Desk is user-centric and common across all technology services. It is the authorized spokesperson and customer face of an IT organization to the end users.

Service Desk performs several important cross-functional activities on behalf of almost every other function in the IT organization, and Service Desk also undertakes the first level support for every issue across all services and technologies.

In our service integration framework, the service desk has a very important role. We also envisage that the role of the service desk in a SIAM-enabled enterprise will be that of a business aligned service desk, who will be proactive and will drive user-centric change adoption across enterprise consumers.

Service Desk in the operation integration context will become the customer experience interface for the entire service value chain, and will perform the following three critical to enable operations integration:

1. **Service Aggregator** – Becoming a SPOC for all enterprise services to the end user. This includes services governed by SIAM which could be delivered in house, hosted, outsourced or cloud models.

2. **Productivity Maximizer** – Become the catalyst for driving increase in user productivity for technology enabled business services by identifying and promoting automation and self-service options for many of the common end user facing activities.

3. **Business Change Advocate** – Become the catalyst to drive adoption and introduction of new services and capabilities which will benefit users. Collate feedback across social and vocal channels and relay this information to the service producers for improving service quality and experience. The Service Desk in context of operation integration would be measured through improved Net Promoter Score (NPS) and increased User Effectiveness Index (UEI).

Command Center

While Service Desk is the SPOC for all end-user reported issues in the organization, the command center is the SPOC for all the CI/Technology originated issues in an IT organization

Command center undertakes monitoring and control of events across all technologies, across end-to-end layers of IT, and manages the lifecycle of event and alerts, and in many cases, critical incident management is facilitated by the command center.

In our integration framework, we have an important role for the command center. With the advent of complex digital enterprises, the role of the command center will become critical for business services.

Availability management and the command center will become the custodians of business service availability. We also envision that the future will evolve towards a unified service desk plus command center as a combined function where the individuals will perform multiple roles.

The command center shall assume and perform the following roles:

1. **Operations Bridge** – Be the single point of contact across all service providers, and service towers that constitute to deliver the business service to the consumer. The bridge would enable information flow and collaboration across all service chain roles, and integrate the feed to the service desk who would handle the end-user perspective.

2. **Situation Manager** –the single point of control to drive resolution of situations which occur. Identify the correct value chain when resolving outages, critical incidents, or service continuity issues, and act as an orchestrator across all service providers in the ecosystem.

3. **Automation Advocate** – Drive operational analytics to identify the automation opportunities for activities which pass through the operations bridge. Analyze situations to suggest preventive and post-facto automated actions, which can be either done at the command center or be orchestrated across the service provider towers to deliver outcomes and improve productivity.

The command center in context of operation integration would be measured on driving increased Automation Index (AI) and Higher Integration Index (HII) across the service provider ecosystem.

7 SERVICE LEVEL MANAGEMENT

It was not that long ago that Service Level Agreements (SLAs) for IT services came into existence. They evolved from the SLAs of tele-communication services in the early 1980s and proliferated with the IT helpdesk in the late 1980s.

The need for a formal SLA was never really felt before that. While telecom SLAs were focused mostly on the quality of the data communication services, helpdesk SLAs were multidimensional in nature. The formalization of an SLA for IT services started with the best practice promoted by the Helpdesk Institute in the early 1990s. The Helpdesk Institute was also focused on the SLAs for support services.

With the widespread adoption of the ITIL framework and best practices, SLAs became a prominent component in the service management domain. An SLA is a formal, written and signed agreement between a service provider and the service consumer or buyer which lists down the agreed aspects of the service – quality, availability, responsibilities, etc.

IT Service Operations Revolve Around SLAs

The intention of agreeing to an SLA is to ensure that both the parties exactly understand what level of service and availability will be provided as part of the relationship.

7 SERVICE LEVEL MANAGEMENT

They are negotiated prior to signing of the contract. If services are provided by the same legal entity, this may not become a legal document or a formal contract, but you still need a formal agreement.

However, when these are agreed with an external supplier, this usually always forms part of a legal contract. At a stage when a contract is being negotiated or is yet to be signed, the supplier tries extremely hard to make a good impression on the client. They want the client to understand and feel that the supplier is the best partner to work with, more often than not with the best intention of the customer in mind.

SLA vs SLO

SLA is a formal, written and signed agreement between a service provider and a client. It lists and describes the services to be provided, who will provide the services, at what frequency, and to what standard. It also lists the metrics by which that service is measured and the remedies or penalties, if service levels are not achieved. Once compiled and agreed, the SLA forms a key point of reference against which the effectiveness or failure of the service provider is measured.

The word 'agreement' has an implied meaning. Synonyms are contract, commitment, arrangement, understanding, and covenant. A legally binding agreement is usually a contract, but an SLA can also be made as a Memorandum of Understanding (MoU) that is not legally enforceable. In most outsourcing deals, SLAs form part of the contract and are legally binding.

A SLO (Service Level Objective) is another term used in lieu of an SLA when the service provider is not willing or unable to accept the contractual obligation or penalties imposed if the SLA is not achieved, but accepts and agrees to the target to provide the service level in good faith. It is also quite common in traditional IT outsourcing deals, to start the engagement with an SLO for a few months before the SLA kicks in.

This is usually done to allow the incoming service providers to get a handle on the environment and increase their knowledge of the business applications, which likely will be a pre-requisite for them to achieve the SLAs. In the 'X-as-a-service' (or XaaS, where "X" could stand for anything) delivery model, this is less common.

7.1 Developing and Managing SLA

How to develop an SLA?

SLAs must be signed with the contract at the beginning of a project. You will still be required to develop SLAs for additional services that may be added at a later stage.

The diagram below (Figure 26) is a self-explanatory method for developing an SLA.

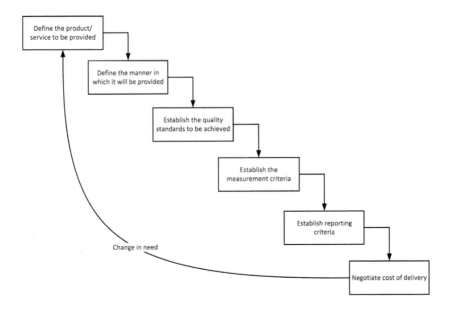

Figure 26: Developing SLA

If you invest more time in developing the SLA for new services, you will waste less time in dealing with subsequent SLA review and amendment discussions with the customer.

7.1.1 SLA Architecture for SLA Gap Analysis

There will always be gaps (and defects) in the established SLAs. Remember, SLAs are not carved on stone and can be changed. To gauge the completeness of the SLA, refer to the architecture diagram (Figure 27) – if all the factors have been designed and covered, then it can be considered as complete.

7 SERVICE LEVEL MANAGEMENT

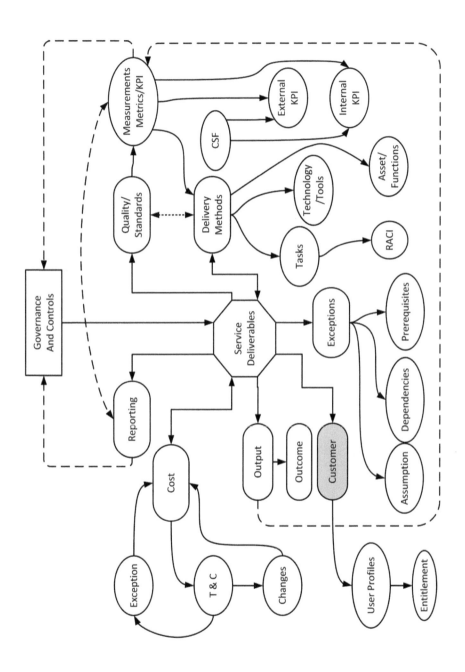

Figure 27: SLA Architecture

Listed below are a few points that would make the SLAs incomplete:

1. **One sided SLAs:** A balanced SLA should provide a platform for both parties to have a successful and mutually beneficial relationship.

2. **Incomplete RACI:** there are responsibilities and accountability on both the sides for an SLA to be met.

3. **KPI (Key Performance Indicators), but no CSF (Critical Success Factor):** It is common to find a big list of KPIs in an outsourcing contract. KPIs do not typically attract penalties, due to which, they do not get the level of attention that they should.

4. **Rationalization in Multi Supplier Environment:** In a multi supplier ecosystem, contracts usually get negotiated at different times, and the dependency between suppliers is often ignored.

5. **No Benchmarks:** It is important to base the SLA on what is achievable.

6. **Inability to Measure:** If you can't measure it, then you can't manage it. SLAs that can't be measured serve no purpose. A supplier will never breach unmeasured SLAs, and the customer loses the ability to ascertain service performance.

7.2 Customer Relationship Management

Despite great performance in the actual service delivery, an SDM will not succeed if he does not manage the relationship with the customer. Lot of factors impact such relationships.

Positive and Negative Third-Party Influence on Customer

Customer also has exposure and access to industry forums and vendor's campaigns, and in fact better exposure than an SDM.

However, the SDM has better exposure to diversified real-life operations and access to proven practices through his peers and real-life learning from other customer environments. Positive influence will work better for you, but beware of negative influence as well. The common influencing parties are:

- **Product Vendor's Influence** – Product Vendors influence customers to sell their products. An SDM must ensure that the customer makes the right decision.

  One very common example is about service management tools. There have been many occasions where ITSM tool vendors have persuaded the customer to opt for out-of-the-box implementation. It is a faulty concept which will hurt the customer's operations, and customers must
- be safeguarded against such faulty concepts.

  Research Analyst Influence – off late, industry analysts are crossing the boundary of their charter. Instead of advising CIOs on making the right decision, they tend to use technology to find the answers.

  To prevent the impact of such decisions on your operations, protect yourself and your customers from wrong decisions. To deal with this situation, keep your organization's point of view or individual PoV handy and ensure that it reflects thought leadership.

Righteous Thing vs. Popular Thing

Often there is a conflict between righteousness and populism. Right things may not be popular. A process-led approach will lead to enforcement of discipline. It is a matter of writing a balanced diet for the health of IT service. You do not eat junk food all the time, but you do not eat boiled vegetables all the time either.

You cannot sustain a bad practice in the long run, and you will be forced to adopt the right things at some point of time. People understand that the rule of law is good to avoid chaos, but that understanding may not be strong enough to enforce discipline. Some parts of the organizations are usually keen to adapt good practices and be disciplined more than others.

For example, in one organization, we implemented a change-management process and linked it to configuration management and the CMDB. A policy statement was signed by all the stakeholders which said that, 'Each RFC must be related to at least one configuration item'. This rule was enforced in the system. Before this enforcement, all use cases were explored—like what if RFC the pertains to a configuration item (CI) that is not available in CMDB—and for each of the use cases, recourse was also established; for example, in this case a generic CI was created.

The manager of the database groups enforced this rule upon his team members, and did not approve any change unless the RFC was related to the database CI (he was in the approval chain for all database changes.)

His team did not like it, but this allowed him to trace incidents on database and relate them to RFCs. Over time, the change-management system had enough data to report what kind of changes could produce what kind of incidents and how to avoid the risks.

In short, the decision-makers in the organization need to make a choice between when to become popular and when to become right. They might have the opportunity to be both right and popular, but that kind of opportunity may not exist all the time.

Note: Use of a generic configuration item CI will act as a measurement of CMDB completeness. If too many RFCs are related to a generic CI, it means that the CMDB is complete or that people are taking the shortcuts.

Follow Me, or Lead Me or Get Out of My Way

7 SERVICE LEVEL MANAGEMENT

Customer is looking for these three options and you need to know the characteristics of your customer and deal accordingly.

- **'Lead Me'**: there are customers who do not know much but are aware of their limitations. Educate them.
- **'Follow Me'**: These are customers who know their areas and are aware of their strengths. Learn from them.
- **'Get out of My Way'**: There are customers who do not know much but believe that they know a lot, and are therefore very difficult to handle. A multi-prong strategy is required to deal with them. Allow them to live under the illusion as long as it does not hurt your operations and SLAs. If it reaches a point where it hurts, collaborate and reason with them.

Customers, who live under illusion, may not be willing to reason. The strategy must focus on evaluating righteousness vs the populism.

In a nutshell, if you neither lead, nor follow, then you are kicked out. It is easy for a customer to kick-out an order taker as compared to a service provider, but customers will not usually consider kicking out a trusted advisor or strategic partner.

Dealing with Unreasonable Customer

Sometimes, an SDM may encounter a stakeholder from the customer's organization who is tough and difficult to deal with. They tend to dictate the procedure based on their point of view, but the SDM may determine that the procedure is not likely to deliver the desired results.

What should the SDM do in that scenario? Should SDM follow the customer and own the accountability of a bad result? This situation requires special handling techniques.

Rely upon the diplomatic techniques and bureaucratic techniques to overcome the situation. Diplomatic techniques will help in avoiding work that is not right.

Every person in a customer organization is not unreasonable. There will be some, but you will find more people who are ready to reason and be logical. You need to form an alliance with logical and reasonable people and press your logic with the support of a larger group.

Bureaucratic technique will have you create evidence of every action you take along with justification for the actions. This could indemnify you from the accountability of a bad result. Finally, it is a matter of choice – being right vs being popular. Determine what is more beneficial for that particular situation.

8 APPENDIX

There is a lot of misunderstanding about the role of a technical analyst (server, network, database, application, middleware etc.) when it comes to service management process.

This section provides details of common service management roles and responsibilities that a technical analyst is expected to undertake.

8.1 Technical Analyst Role in ITSM Processes

Incident Management

Incident Resolver – An incident resolver is a subject matter expert for a specific technology, and has the below mentioned responsibilities pertaining to Incident Management.

- Review and accept incidents assigned to their support group. This includes validating the scope of support, prioritization and categorization.

- Investigation may include the utilization of advanced technical scripts, diagnostic tools and utilities and specific KB articles accessible to expert support groups.expert support groups.

- Interface with third party Vendors' technical support when required for Incident Investigation & Diagnosis.

- Diagnose, investigate and apply resolution to restore services.

- Record complete information about the issue, symptoms, chronology of events and activities performed throughout the Incident Lifecycle.

- Participate in major incident investigation when engaged. Join bridge calls and group chats for MIM in a timely manner. Provide technical contribution for post incident reports.

Problem Management

Problem Identifier – this role is usually played by designated subject matter experts from each technology and they are responsible for creating problem records when issues that qualify as problems are detected within their technology domain.

Problem Investigator – this role is usually played by senior subject matter experts from each technology, and they have the below mentioned responsibilities:

- Review and accept problems assigned to their support group. This includes validating the scope of support, and reviewing problem inputs such as major incident reports.

- Work with other technical support groups, OEMs and third-party vendors when required for investigation & diagnosis.

- Produce RCA reports and/or participate in RCA review meetings with the problem manager and other key stakeholders.

- Record complete information about the issue, symptoms, chronology of events and activities performed throughout the problem lifecycle.

Change Management

Change Requester – this role can be played by IT personnel who require changes to be implemented. This role has the following responsibilities

- Raise change requests, including all the required and mandatory details and technical justification for change.

- Adhere to change management lead time requirements, and controls such as planned maintenance windows and change moratorium periods.

Change Implementer – this role is played by subject matter experts from the change implementation group, and they have the below mentioned responsibilities:

- Discuss the change in the technical advisory board (TAB) and ensure that technical considerations are reviewed. Represent the change in the CAB meeting, and answer any questions to facilitate risk and impact assessment, scheduling and other considerations.

- The change implementer should complete all the tasks assigned directly to them, and coordinate with other teams if there are dependent tasks assigned to other teams as part of implementation.

- Update the change record with the implementation results, and set the change to 'Completed' status.

- Produce PIR reports for failed changes, emergency changes and any other type of change where a PIR is dictated as per the process.

- Participate in PIR review meetings.

Capacity Management

Capacity Analyst – this role is responsible for applying detailed technical knowledge pertaining to their technology area to perform Capacity Monitoring, Analysis, and Tuning.

- Perform technical analysis on monitoring data extracted from monitoring tools on resource usage, produce capacity analysis reports for capacity optimization.

- Evaluate tuning options and recommend tuning solutions.

- Identify areas of under/over Capacity and champion recommendations to address capacity issues.

Asset and Configuration Management

Technical CI Owner - is anyone who owns a configuration item and has been identified as the CI owner in the CMDB. The CI Owner will typically be the lead of the support group that manages the CI.

- Ensures that the technical attributes of all assets and configuration items owned are registered in the configuration management database correctly

Availability Management

Availability Risk Analyst - is responsible for applying detailed technical knowledge pertaining to their technology area to perform Availability Monitoring, Data Collection, and Analysis etc.

- Perform availability and performance health check on IT systems and components.

- Identify single points of failure and champion recommendations to address availability issues.

- Ensure that availability is designed into services and applications right from the outset when the service is initially conceptualized.

Request Fulfillment

Request Fulfiller - this role is usually played by a member of a fulfiller group from each technology, and carries the below mentioned responsibilities:

Responsibilities

- Review service requests and fulfillment tasks which are assigned to their fulfillment group.

- Fulfill approved and authorized Service Requests as defined by the process.

- Update the Service Request ticket throughout the fulfillment lifecycle, and share relevant details with the requester upon the fulfillment of the request.

- Perform technical analysis on monitoring data extracted from monitoring tools on resource usage, produce capacity analysis reports for capacity optimization.

- Evaluate tuning options and recommend tuning solutions.

- Identify areas of under capacity or over capacity and champion recommendations to address capacity issues.

ABOUT THE AUTHORS

Jagadeshwar Gattu

Jagadeshwar Gattu (Jags) is the Corporate Vice President of HCL Technologies, a US$ 8.2 billion global technology company. Jagadeshwar leads Infrastructure Service Delivery, Americas.

Jags is helping corporates to transform their businesses by providing IT solutions and running operations. He is responsible for setting a strategic direction, service delivery, industrializing operations and bringing in automation and process maturity.

Jags is part of HCL's core team that forayed into the then unchartered Global Remote Management space. He is a strategic thinker with a pragmatic approach to implementation and strongly believes in driving vision into reality.

Over the years Jags has held various leadership positions at HCL and his expertise is not only limited to Service Delivery, Transition, Transformation and Leadership Development, but also delivering operational standardization through DRYiCE Autonomics & Orchestration framework & Workforce Transformation.

Prior to his tenure at HCL, Jags co-founded an Identity and Access Management firm, ILANTUS Technologies.

In his free time, Jags likes to spend time in spiritual activities and in exploring nature. He is an avid traveler and enjoys spending time with his family.

Prafull Verma

Prafull Verma has a bachelor's degree in electronics and communication engineering and has over thirty years of experience in the area of electronic data processing and Information Technology. He started his career in India in electronic data processing systems and later moved to the United States in 1997. Over the past 30 years, he has worked on diversified areas in computer science and information technologies. Some of his key experience areas are design and implementation of heterogeneous networks, midrange technical support management, end-user service design and management, and the implementation and management of process-driven ITSM systems.

Prafull has acquired a unique blend of expertise in integrated areas of tools, process, governance, operations, and technology. He is the author of several methodology and frameworks for IT service management that include multi-vendor ITIL frameworks, ITSM for cloud computing and Service Integration.

Prafull's competencies and specializations include merging engineering with service management, and outsourcing business management.

Currently, Prafull is working for HCL Technologies Ltd. as Fellow and Chief Architect and is responsible for architecting, designing, and building next generation service management products, and delivering services and solutions around digital service management platforms. He is also serving as a governing board member of The Open Group.

ABOUT THE AUTHORS

Kalyan Kumar

Kalyan Kumar (KK) is the Chief Technology Officer for HCL Technologies, and leads all Global Technology Practices. In his current role, Kalyan is responsible for defining Architecture & Technology Strategy, New Solutions Development and Engineering across all Enterprise Infrastructure, Business Productivity, Unified Communications and Collaboration, Enterprise Platforms and DevOps Service Lines. Kalyan is also responsible for business and service delivery for Cross Functional Services for HCL across the globe.

Kalyan is widely acknowledged as an expert and path-breaker on BSM/ITSM and IT Architecture and Cloud Platforms, and has developed several IPs for the company in these domains. He is also credited with building the HCL MTaaS service from scratch – which has a multi-million turnover today and acts a proprietary benchmark for Global IT Infrastructure Services Delivery.

His team is also credited with developing the MyCloud SM platform for Cloud Service Management & My DevOps, which is a pioneering breakthrough in the Utility Computing and Hybrid Agile Ops Model space. He has been presented with many internal and external awards for his thought leadership in IT Management.

Kalyan also runs the HCL ISD IPDEV Incubator Group where he is responsible for incubating new services, platforms and IPs for the company. He is also active in the Digital Systems Integration Roadmap and Solutions Strategy for HCL.

Kalyan has spoken at many prestigious industry platforms and is currently actively engaged in Partner Advisory Board of CA Technologies, and IBM Software.

In his free time, Kalyan likes to jam with his band 'Contraband' as a drummer and percussionist, and reviews consumer technology gadgets.

He can be followed on Twitter @KKLIVE and at LinkedIn http://www.linkedin.com/in/kalyankumar

FROM THE SAME AUTHOR(S)

Adapting to Digital Transformation: Design Sensible SLAs for Modern IT
Authored By – Prafull Verma, Mohan Kewalramani, and Kalyan Kumar

Paperback: 188 pages
Language: English
ISBN-10: 0692889167
ISBN-13: 978-0692889169
Dimensions: 6 x 0.4 x 9 inches

Most enterprises follow the ITIL framework to design, deliver, and operate IT services, which includes developing Service Level Agreements (SLAs). These are however associated with technical services, which are not outlined in the guidance provided by ITIL. Although it seems relatively straight forward and easy, the reality is that there are many pitfalls and misconceptions in developing a set of meaningful SLAs that will work seamlessly in a multi-supplier environment.

Additionally, the Information Technology landscape is changing rapidly with the emergence of disruptive new technologies underpinned by the Cloud. New business models are evolving in the creation and delivering of IT Services. In the modern world of XaaS - anything and everything as-a-service, traditional methods and practices are incompatible and need to be optimized, including SLAs, while still supporting large portions of legacy environments that continue to exist in enterprises. This book provides guidance on the factors to consider when developing SLAs in a traditional as well as modern IT service environment, and highlights the common perils to watch out for.

FROM THE SAME AUTHOR(S)

Foundation for XaaS: Service Architecture in the 21st Century Enterprise

Authored by Prafull Verma and Kalyan Kumar

List Price: $12.95
6" x 9" (15.24 x 22.86 cm)
Black & White on White paper
152 pages
ISBN-13: 978-0692688311 (Custom Universal)
ISBN-10: 0692688315
BISAC: Computers / Information Technology

XaaS is a collective term said to stand for several things including "X as a-service". Everything (and anything!) as-a-service is a rapidly expanding model not only in cloud services, but also in every other industry. It grew from a utility service model and applied to IT and now non-IT services as well.

This is the new delivery model and warrants a new approach to service management, and also requires a new approach to design and publish a service. Like service management architecture that we discussed in our earlier publication, service architecture is largely an ignored aspect in service design. IT professionals talk more about application architecture than service architecture. This book discusses the sets of service properties that collectively form a service architecture and then also talks about the building blocks of XaaS service management system.

Foundation of Intelligent IT Operations: CMDB and Service Maps

Authored by Mr. Prafull Verma, Mr. Mohan Kewalramani, and Mr. Kalyan Kumar

List Price: $15.95
6" x 9" (15.24 x 22.86 cm)
Black & White on White paper172 pages
ISBN-13: 978-0692380925 (Custom Universal)
ISBN-10: 0692380922
BISAC: Computers / Information Technology

The scale of enterprise IT environments are growing rapidly and computing resources are deployed in abundance. Consequently, management of IT operations gets increasingly complex. Service Maps and the CMDB are key tools to enable an organization to intelligently manage the complexity of dependencies and relationships between components. Theoretically, this sounds reasonable and easily achievable, especially since the concept of a CMDB was introduced in ITIL v2 more than a decade ago, and the assumption is that almost all the organizations that have adopted ITIL would have a CMDB and will be delivering on its intended objectives. The reality is far removed from theory though.

Designing, implementing, and maintaining a sensible CMDB that is fit for purpose, without turning into a failed project requires more than just theoretical knowledge. Additionally, with the rapid adoption of cloud computing, Internet of Things (IoT), and other disruptive technologies in an increasingly complex multi-supplier environment with "Service Integration and Management (SIAM)", the old school vision of the CMDB needs to be revisited with a renewed perspective to keep it relevant to our IT environments today.

FROM THE SAME AUTHOR(S)

Software Asset Management: Understanding and Implementing an Optimal Solution

Authored by Mr. Prafull Verma and Mr. Kalyan Kumar

List Price: $15.95
6" x 9" (15.24 x 22.86 cm)
Black & White on White paper 148 pages
ISBN-13: 978-0692324264 (Custom Universal)
ISBN-10: 0692324267
BISAC: Computers / Information Technology
ion Technology

Software Asset Management (SAM) is an essential need for all IT organizations, not just because of the cost of so ware but also because of the potential litigation of copyright violation for the use of unlicensed so ware. Most of the organizations deploy tools for so ware asset management, but fail to achieve the desired goals because tools are a small part of the holistic solution. is book explains the underlying complexity of SAM and includes all aspects of SAM solution that includes solution architecture, the SAM processes, tools and function and provide a guideline to develop, build and operate an optimal solution.

Service Integration: A Practical Guide to Multivendor Service Management

Authored by Prafull Verma, and Kalyan Kumar

List Price: $15.95
5.5" x 8.5" (13.97 x 21.59 cm)
Black & White on White paper 148 pages
ISBN-13: 978-0692219959 (Custom Universal)
ISBN-10: 0692219951
BISAC: Computers / Information Technology

This book is intended to present a simplified guide for IT generalists who are new to the service integration subject. The purpose of this book is to educate IT professionals with the basic concepts of service integration. Additionally, the purpose is to provide core guidance to Service Management professionals, upon which they can build and implement the service integration management framework in their environment.

Foundation of IT Operations Management: Event Monitoring and Controls

Authored by Prafull Verma, and Kalyan Kumar

List Price: $15.95
6" x 9" (15.24 x 22.86 cm)
Black & White on White paper 138 pages
Foundation of IT Operation
ISBN-13: 978-0692205709 (Custom Universal)
ISBN-10: 0692205705
BISAC: Computers / Information Technology

In IT operations, event monitoring and control - where you continuously monitor the health of IT

FROM THE SAME AUTHOR(S)

There is a lot of guidance available on technology management in IT industry but this book is focusing on technology independent service management. The book addresses to all the IT people from a process practitioner perspective, however, the fundamentals are presented in simplistic terms, and therefore it should be useful to all the IT people.

It will describe the process engineering concept and how it can be applied to IT Service Management. This is not just about the industry standard framework such as ITIL and COBIT, but about the common processes that are generally used in real life operations. This book does not focus on any technology.

Printed in Poland
by Amazon Fulfillment
Poland Sp. z o.o., Wrocław